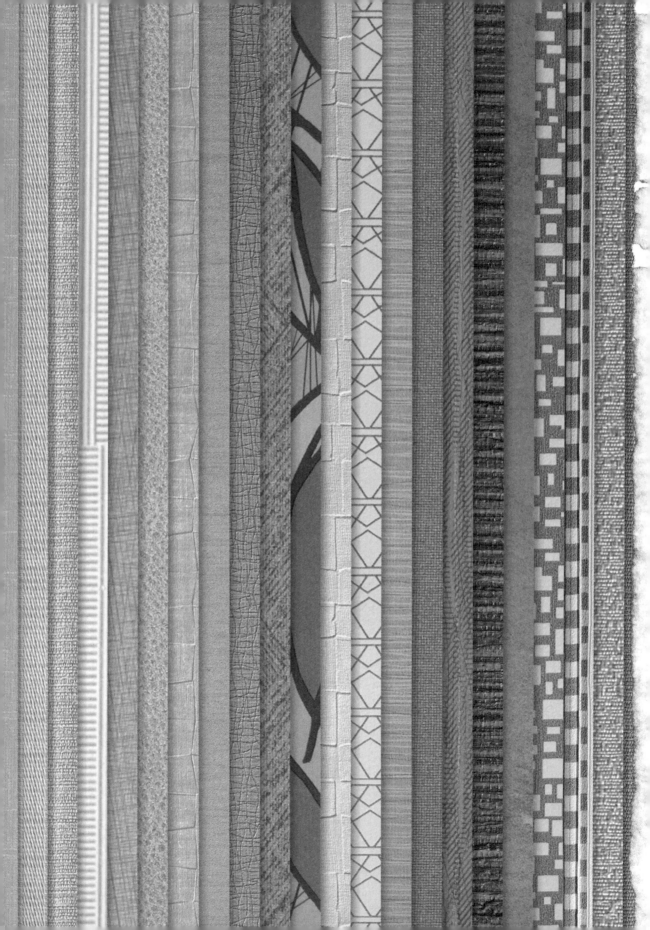

WOLF-GORDON

SAMPLE BOOK

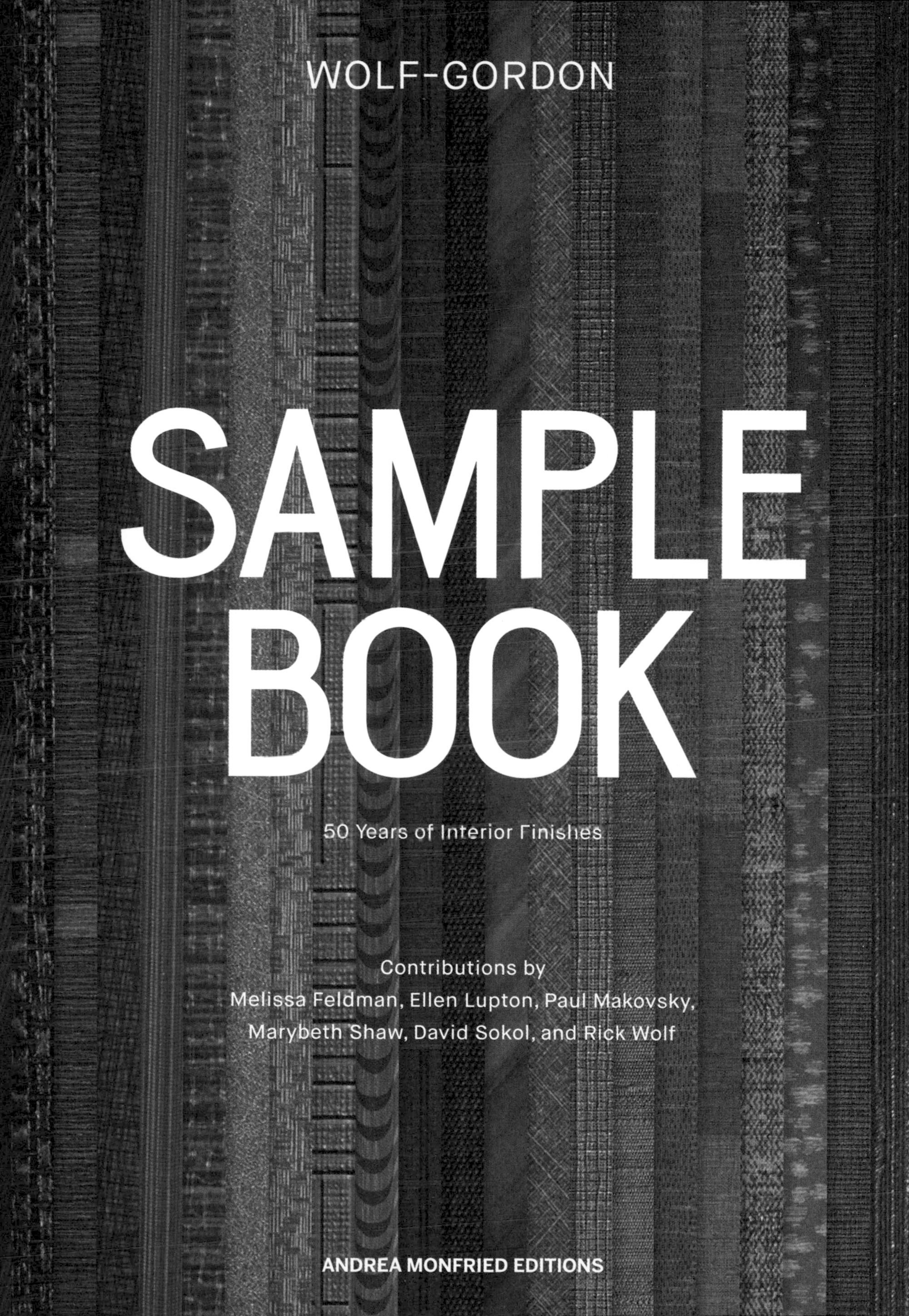

WOLF-GORDON

SAMPLE BOOK

50 Years of Interior Finishes

Contributions by
Melissa Feldman, Ellen Lupton, Paul Makovsky,
Marybeth Shaw, David Sokol, and Rick Wolf

ANDREA MONFRIED EDITIONS

CONTENTS

PREFACE

You may have once worked at a company where photographs of a parent- or grandparent-founder could be glimpsed on a wall of the president's office. You may have seen a generation of owners grow up in the business, working their way through different departments and gaining a unique understanding of operations. You knew the owners by first name, and they committed themselves to you through good and bad economies alike. Despite changes in actual ownership, Wolf-Gordon remains this family company... but with a difference.

When Rick Wolf, David Gordon, and Rob Wolf took on roles as CEO, executive vice president, and CFO, Wolf-Gordon reinvented itself as a place of design, opportunity, and entrepreneurship. With the fiftieth anniversary of the company's 1967 founding on the horizon, we decided to celebrate in a book the distinctive warmth, passion, energy, humor, and dedication that Rick, David, and Rob have fostered among the entire team.

Since design companies introduce products by way of a sample book, and since, in fact, Wolf-Gordon was founded on a sample book, we could not find a more appropriate inspiration. The structure of *Wolf-Gordon: Sample Book* reflects the polyvalent spirit of this enterprise. Our combination of products, projects, and personalities has generated a brand that is youthful and wise, daring and dependable. We all look forward to many more years of delighting our customers and contributing to commercial interior design from this platform of challenge and opportunity.

Creating this book has been a complicated and labor-intensive but tremendously valuable process, made a pleasure by the expert planning, conceptual strength, management, and friendship of publisher Andrea Monfried. It has also provided an opportunity to work with our dear partners in design, karlssonwilker. Hjalti Karlsson has been at the helm on this project. Through the years, we have worked with many talented photographers, but James Shanks stands out. He is our principal collaborator on product and installation shots, and we are grateful for his beautiful work and cheerful responsiveness. Finally, the photographic coordination and administrative tasks associated with *Sample Book* have been enthusiastically borne by the intelligent, meticulous, and dedicated professionals on the Wolf-Gordon marketing team.

Marybeth Shaw
Vice President, Design and Marketing

INTRODUCTION

The company that Bernie Gordon and my father, Mel Wolf, founded fifty years ago was a product of its time. Even though today we look at midcentury America as a golden age of design, back then success was defined by consumption of goods. The Wolf-Gordon of the late 1960s plugged into this commodity mind-set. And while the company enjoyed impressive revenue, its methods for selling wallcovering—dealing with many of the same wholesale sources that supplied competitors, differentiating products with little more than a label, and avoiding inventory positions—lacked a conceptual framework and do not define success in the present-day market.

Wolf-Gordon has evolved dramatically since 1967. Product is no longer a euphemism for mere goods.

Every item in our catalog is a result of invention, research, and testing. With a dedication to high performance and high style, our work can be summed up simply as *design*. And while the book you are holding honors Wolf-Gordon's roots, what it really recognizes is our transformation.

Just as I've drawn a distinction between commodity and designed product, I choose the word "our" with the utmost care. No one person redefined Wolf-Gordon. David Gordon, Rob Wolf, and I hired key people whose expertise we trusted, and we gave them leeway to exercise their talent and knowledge. While our personalities would not have allowed any other kind of executive decision-making, the three of us are still astounded by the creativity and tirelessness with which each member of the Wolf-Gordon family has embraced this management style.

Because business reflects its time, the credit for Wolf-Gordon's transformation can be shared with many, not just those within the company. The changes that have taken place inside Wolf-Gordon mirror Americans' ever-increasing design savvy. More people than ever can sense when a lobby or an office is more than a vanilla box, and they know that that effect is possible only when every square inch has undergone a design process.

My father would have been surprised by the parallel metamorphosis of Wolf-Gordon and its customer

Tony Prota (second from left), Mel Wolf (third from left), Bernie Gordon (third from right), Frank Carr (second from right), c. 1965

Rick Wolf, Mel Wolf, Bernie Gordon, David Gordon (left to right), 1998

base of commercial interior designers. Indeed, he was not one to be consumed by design. Mel entered the wallcovering business during the Depression. When he was fourteen, an acquaintance got him a job in the Gilford, Inc., fabrics warehouse to supplement his single mother's seamstress income. Dad then worked his way up.

To be sure, investing in experimentation and accumulating inventory would make Mel bristle, but the beauty of a genuine design business is that it both reflects and proposes new thinking for its time. And it's often this progressiveness that creates desire in interior design specifiers. If Mel and Bernie were salesmen through and through, something I've learned from thirty-three years at Wolf-Gordon is that there is no better driver of sales than emotion. Of that, they would approve.

On behalf of everyone here, I am privileged to share our journey and these lessons with you.

Rick Wolf
President and CEO

PRODUCTS

1967–1996

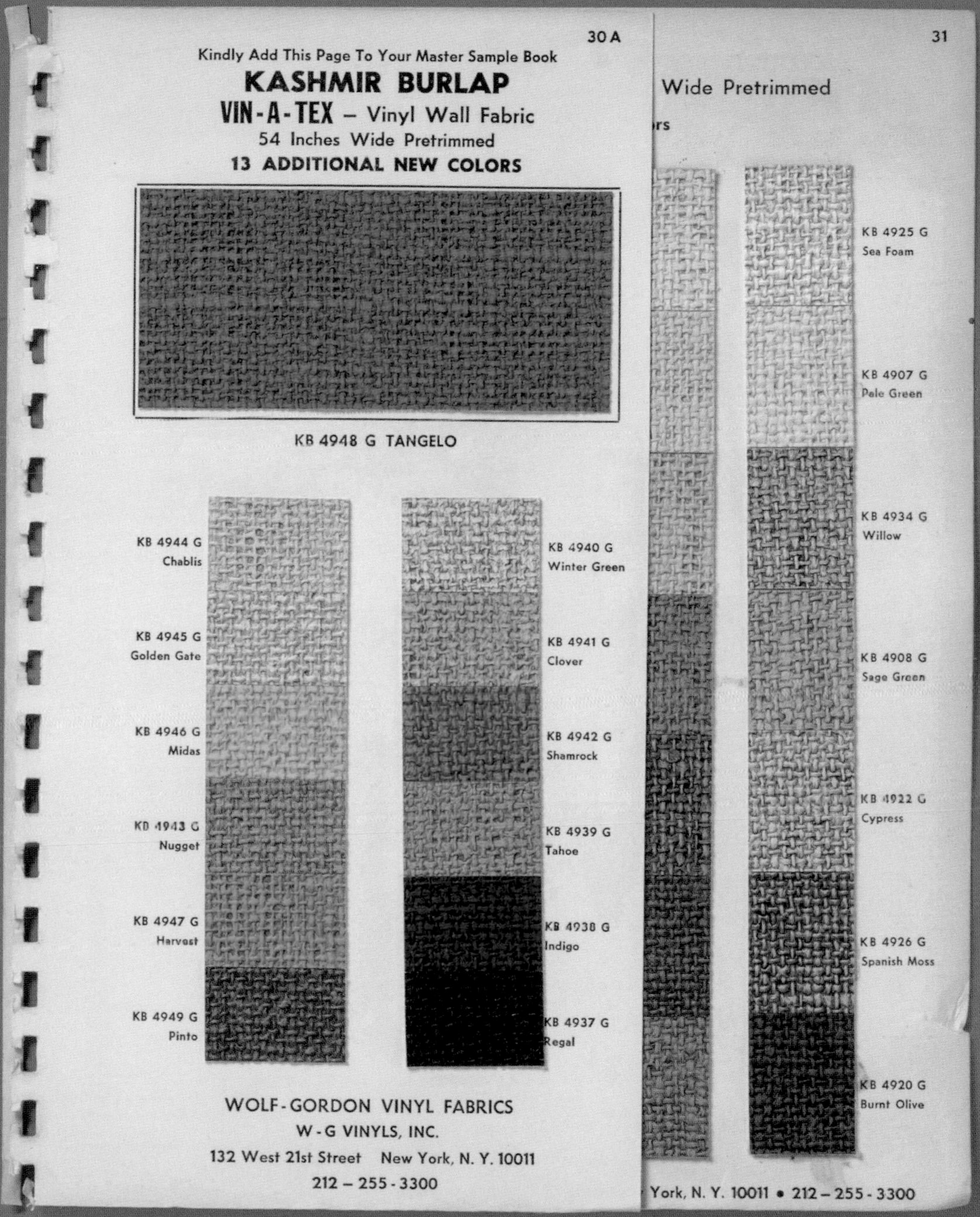

Kindly Add This Page To Your Master Sample Book

KASHMIR BURLAP
VIN-A-TEX — Vinyl Wall Fabric
54 Inches Wide Pretrimmed
13 ADDITIONAL NEW COLORS

Wide Pretrimmed

ors

KB 4948 G TANGELO

KB 4925 G
Sea Foam

KB 4907 G
Pale Green

KB 4934 G
Willow

KB 4944 G
Chablis

KB 4940 G
Winter Green

KB 4945 G
Golden Gate

KB 4941 G
Clover

KB 4908 G
Sage Green

KB 4946 G
Midas

KB 4942 G
Shamrock

KB 4943 G
Nugget

KB 4939 G
Tahoe

KB 4922 G
Cypress

KB 4947 G
Harvest

KB 4938 G
Indigo

KB 4926 G
Spanish Moss

KB 4949 G
Pinto

KB 4937 G
Regal

KB 4920 G
Burnt Olive

WOLF-GORDON VINYL FABRICS
W-G VINYLS, INC.
132 West 21st Street   New York, N. Y. 10011
212 – 255 - 3300

York, N. Y. 10011 • 212 – 255 - 3300

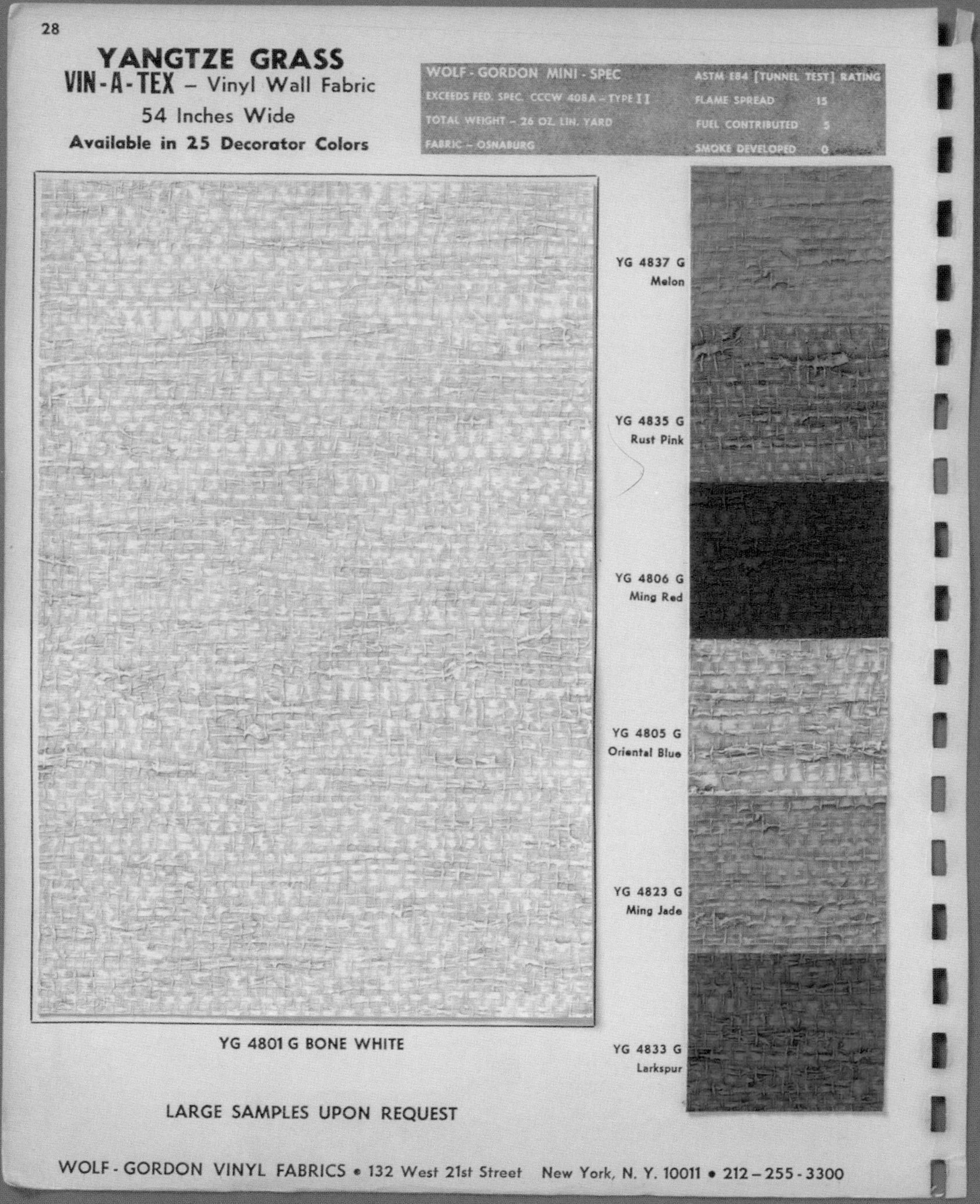

YANGTZE GRASS
VIN-A-TEX – Vinyl Wall Fabric
54 Inches Wide
Available in 25 Decorator Colors

WOLF-GORDON MINI-SPEC		ASTM E84 [TUNNEL TEST] RATING	
EXCEEDS FED. SPEC. CCCW 408A – TYPE II		FLAME SPREAD	15
TOTAL WEIGHT – 26 OZ. LIN. YARD		FUEL CONTRIBUTED	5
FABRIC – OSNABURG		SMOKE DEVELOPED	0

YG 4837 G
Melon

YG 4835 G
Rust Pink

YG 4806 G
Ming Red

YG 4805 G
Oriental Blue

YG 4823 G
Ming Jade

YG 4833 G
Larkspur

YG 4801 G BONE WHITE

LARGE SAMPLES UPON REQUEST

WOLF-GORDON VINYL FABRICS • 132 West 21st Street   New York, N. Y. 10011 • 212-255-3300

YANGTZE GRASS
VIN-A-TEX — Vinyl Wall Fabric — 54 Inches Wide
Available in 25 Decorator Colors

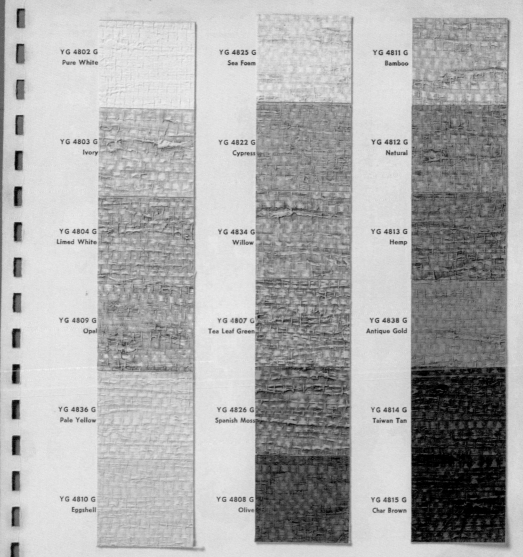

YG 4802 G Pure White	YG 4825 G Sea Foam	YG 4811 G Bamboo
YG 4803 G Ivory	YG 4822 G Cypress	YG 4812 G Natural
YG 4804 G Limed White	YG 4834 G Willow	YG 4813 G Hemp
YG 4809 G Opal	YG 4807 G Tea Leaf Green	YG 4838 G Antique Gold
YG 4836 G Pale Yellow	YG 4826 G Spanish Moss	YG 4814 G Taiwan Tan
YG 4810 G Eggshell	YG 4808 G Olive	YG 4815 G Char Brown

LARGE SAMPLES UPON REQUEST

WOLF-GORDON VINYL FABRICS • 132 West 21st Street New York, N. Y. 10011 • 212-255-3300

WOLF-GORDON
Vinyl Wall Fabric
53-54 Inches Wide

WOLF-GORDON MINI-SPEC	ASTM E84 (Tunnel Test) RATING	
EXCEEDS FED. SPEC. CCCW 408A - TYPE I	FLAME SPREAD	10
TOTAL WEIGHT: 15 OZ. LIN. YARD	FUEL CONTRIBUTED	0
FABRIC: SHEETING	SMOKE DEVELOPED	0

HAITI

HAT 12185 F   MINK

AFRICANA

AF 12170 F   BARLEY

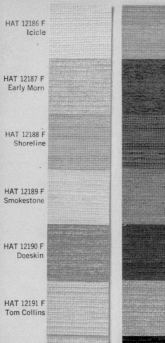

HAT 12186 F
Icicle

HAT 12187 F
Early Morn

HAT 12188 F
Shoreline

HAT 12189 F
Smokestone

HAT 12190 F
Doeskin

HAT 12191 F
Tom Collins

HAT 12192 F
Sunbelt

HAT 12193 F
Heatwave

HAT 12194 F
Burnt Orange

HAT 12195 F
Sugar Cane

HAT 12196 F
Light Cocoa

HAT 12197 F
Rusty

HAT 12198 F
Sky

HAT 12199 F
Midnight

AF 12171 F
Smoke

AF 12172 F
Egg Nog

AF 12173 F
Summer Haze

AF 12174 F
Mustard

AF 12175 F
Cane

AF 12176 F
Whole Wheat

AF 12177 F
Clay

AF 12178 F
Fruitwood

AF 12179 F
Bittersweet

AF 12180 F
Sunshine

AF 12181 F
Dried Grass

AF 12182 F
String

AF 12183 F
Capri Blue

AF 12184 F
Palisade

LARGE SAMPLES UPON REQUEST
Small samples on Haiti & Africana are sampled incorrectly — Should be vertical as per large samples.

WOLF-GORDON
Vinyl Wall Fabric
53-54 Inches Wide

WOLF-GORDON MINI-SPEC	ASTM E84 (Tunnel Test) RATING	
EXCEEDS FED. SPEC. CCCW 408A - TYPE I	FLAME SPREAD	10
TOTAL WEIGHT: 11 OZ. LIN. YARD	FUEL CONTRIBUTED	0
FABRIC: SHEETING	SMOKE DEVELOPED	0

KNOXVILLE

KX 12150 F   SAPPHIRE

KX 12151 F White	KX 12158 F Nugget
KX 12152 F Champagne	KX 12159 F Deep Gold
KX 12153 F Bamboo	KX 12160 F Flame
KX 12154 F Citron	KX 12161 F Cinnamon
KX 12155 F Quartz	KX 12162 F Monarch
KX 12156 F Corn	KX12163 F Flower Pot
KX 12157 F Grain	KX 12164 F Tobacco

OMAHA

OH 12135 F   BEIGE

OH 12136 F Grey	OH 12141 F Sahara
OH 12137 F Antique	OH 12142 F Lioness
OH 12135 F Beige	OH 12143 F Butterscotch
OH 12138 F Primrose	OH 12144 F Autumn Leafs
OH 12139 F Gunny Sack	OH 12145 F Royal Palm
OH 12140 F Ash	OH 12146 F Larkspur

LARGE SAMPLES UPON REQUEST

W-G VINYLS INC.   •   **132 West 21st Street   New York, N.Y. 10011**   •   **(212) 255-3300**

SERGEANT CHEVRON
Vinyl Wall Fabric
53-54 Inches Wide

WOLF-GORDON MINI-SPEC		ASTM E84 (Tunnel Test) RATING	
EXCEEDS FED. SPEC. CCCW 408A - TYPE I		FLAME SPREAD	20
TOTAL WEIGHT: 13 OZ. LIN. YARD		FUEL CONTRIBUTED	0
FABRIC: SCRIM		SMOKE DEVELOPED	10

SC 12300 F   PARCHMENT

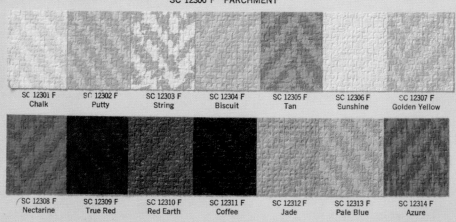

SC 12301 F Chalk	SC 12302 F Putty	SC 12303 F String	SC 12304 F Biscuit	SC 12305 F Tan	SC 12306 F Sunshine	SC 12307 F Golden Yellow

SC 12308 F Nectarine	SC 12309 F True Red	SC 12310 F Red Earth	SC 12311 F Coffee	SC 12312 F Jade	SC 12313 F Pale Blue	SC 12314 F Azure

LARGE SAMPLES UPON REQUEST

W-G VINYLS INC. • 132 West 21st Street New York, N.Y. 10011 • (212) 255-3300

HIGH SOCIETY PATENT

Vinyl Wall & Upholstery Fabric

54 Inches Wide

WOLF-GORDON MINI-SPEC
TOTAL WEIGHT: 30 OZ. LIN. YARD
FABRIC: POLYESTER BACKING
FLAME SPREAD: 20

HS 9756 F   CHIN RED

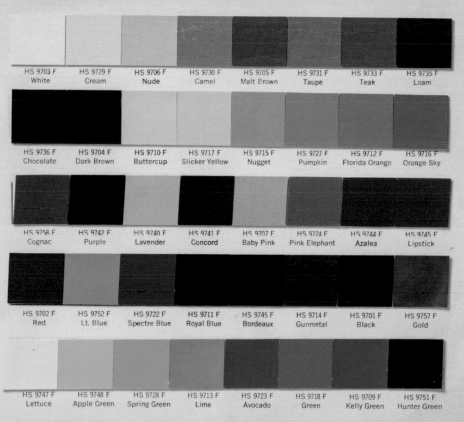

HS 9703 F White	HS 9729 F Cream	HS 9706 F Nude	HS 9730 F Camel	HS 9705 F Malt Brown	HS 9731 F Taupe	HS 9733 F Teak	HS 9735 F Loam
HS 9736 F Chocolate	HS 9704 F Dark Brown	HS 9710 F Buttercup	HS 9717 F Slicker Yellow	HS 9715 F Nugget	HS 9727 F Pumpkin	HS 9712 F Florida Orange	HS 9716 F Orange Sky
HS 9758 F Cognac	HS 9742 F Purple	HS 9740 F Lavender	HS 9741 F Concord	HS 9707 F Baby Pink	HS 9724 F Pink Elephant	HS 9744 F Azalea	HS 9745 F Lipstick
HS 9702 F Red	HS 9752 F Lt. Blue	HS 9722 F Spectre Blue	HS 9711 F Royal Blue	HS 9745 F Bordeaux	HS 9714 F Gunmetal	HS 9701 F Black	HS 9757 F Gold
HS 9747 F Lettuce	HS 9748 F Apple Green	HS 9728 F Spring Green	HS 9713 F Lime	HS 9723 F Avocado	HS 9718 F Green	HS 9709 F Kelly Green	HS 9751 F Hunter Green

W-G VINYLS INC.   •   132 West 21st Street   New York, N.Y. 10011   •   (212) 255-3300

WOLF-GORDON
Vinyl Wall & Upholstery Fabric
52-53 Inches Wide

WOLF-GORDON MINI-SPEC
TOTAL WEIGHT: 25-27 OZ. LIN. YARD
FABRIC: ELASTIC BACKED

LIZARD

AUSSIE OSTRICH

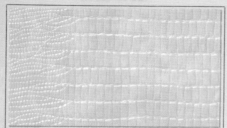

LZ 9650 F   ANTIQUE WHITE — Flame Spread 20

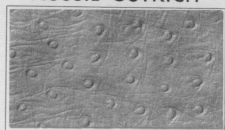

AO 3936 F   BUTTERSCOTCH

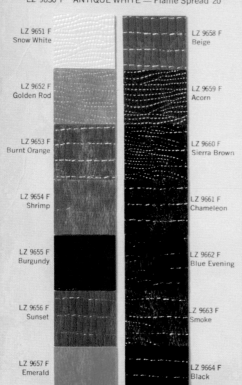

LZ 9651 F Snow White

LZ 9652 F Golden Rod

LZ 9653 F Burnt Orange

LZ 9654 F Shrimp

LZ 9655 F Burgundy

LZ 9656 F Sunset

LZ 9657 F Emerald

LZ 9658 F Beige

LZ 9659 F Acorn

LZ 9660 F Sierra Brown

LZ 9661 F Chameleon

LZ 9662 F Blue Evening

LZ 9663 F Smoke

LZ 9664 F Black

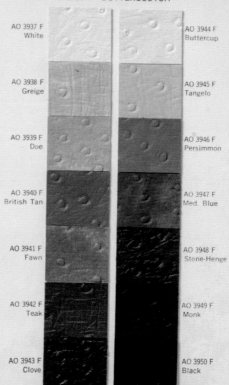

AO 3937 F White

AO 3938 F Greige

AO 3939 F Doe

AO 3940 F British Tan

AO 3941 F Fawn

AO 3942 F Teak

AO 3943 F Clove

AO 3944 F Buttercup

AO 3945 F Tangelo

AO 3946 F Persimmon

AO 3947 F Med. Blue

AO 3948 F Stone-Henge

AO 3949 F Monk

AO 3950 F Black

LARGE SAMPLES UPON REQUEST
W-G VINYLS INC. • 132 West 21st Street New York, N.Y. 10011 • (212) 255-3300

MIDAS MYLAR

Vinyl Wall Fabric

6700 SERIES - 54 Inches Wide

WOLF-GORDON MINI-SPEC	ASTM E84 (Tunnel Test) RATING	
EXCEEDS FED. SPEC. CCCW 408-A TYPE II	FLAME SPREAD	15
TOTAL WEIGHT: 25-26 OZ. LIN. YD.	FUEL CONTRIBUTED	0
FABRIC: POLYESTER BACKING	SMOKE DEVELOPED	45

MM 6710 F Silver	MM 6711 F Gold	MM 6714 F Pewter	MM 6712 F Copper	MM 6715 F Brass	MM 6713 F Brushed Silk

MIDAS MYLAR

Vinyl Wall Fabric

54 Inches Wide

WOLF-GORDON MINI-SPEC	ASTM E84 (Tunnel Test) RATING	
EXCEEDS FED. SPEC. CCCW 408A - TYPE I	FLAME SPREAD	15
TOTAL WEIGHT: 14-15 OZ. LIN. YARD	FUEL CONTRIBUTED	5
FABRIC: POLYESTER	SMOKE DEVELOPED	15

MM 5626 F Flute	MM 5637 F Alumesh	MM 5629 F Ceylon	MM 5638 F Tile	MM 5640 F Puff Diamond	MM 5628 F Deep Crush	MM 5623 F Kid	MM 5639 F Basket

BOA MYLAR

Vinyl Wall Fabric

52-54 Inches Wide

WOLF-GORDON MINI-SPEC	ASTM E84 (Tunnel Test) RATING	
EXCEEDS FED. SPEC. CCCW 408A - TYPE II	FLAME SPREAD	15
TOTAL WEIGHT: 20-21 OZ. LIN. YARD	FUEL CONTRIBUTED	0
FABRIC: POLYESTER BACKING	SMOKE DEVELOPED	15

BOM 5301 F Silver	BOM 5302 F Gunmetal	BOM 5303 F Bronze	BOM 5304 F Gold	BOM 5305 F Pink	BOM 5306 F Red	BOM 5307 F Light Blue	BOM 5308 F Dark Blue	BOM 5309 F Green

LARGE SAMPLES UPON REQUEST   **WOLF-GORDON VINYL FABRICS**

W-G VINYLS INC. • 132 West 21st Street New York, N.Y. 10011 • (212) 255-3300

VALIANT SUEDE

Wallcovering & Upholstery Fabric

53-54 Inches Wide

WOLF-GORDON MINI-SPEC	ASTM E84 (Tunnel Test) RATING	
TOTAL WEIGHT: 30 OZ. LIN. YARD	FLAME SPREAD	20
FABRIC: POLY-COTTON ELASTIC BACKED	FUEL CONTRIBUTED	15
	SMOKE DEVELOPED	25

VS 2357 F RATTAN

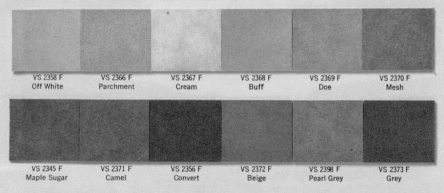

VS 2358 F	VS 2366 F	VS 2367 F	VS 2368 F	VS 2369 F	VS 2370 F
Off White	Parchment	Cream	Buff	Doe	Mesh

VS 2345 F	VS 2371 F	VS 2356 F	VS 2372 F	VS 2398 F	VS 2373 F
Maple Sugar	Camel	Convert	Beige	Pearl Grey	Grey

This new vinyl fabric has all the unique features of Genuine Suede creating variable panel effects.

LARGE SAMPLES UPON REQUEST

W-G VINYLS INC. • **132 West 21st Street New York, N.Y. 10011** • **(212) 255-3300**

VALIANT SUEDE — 61 Standard Stock Colors

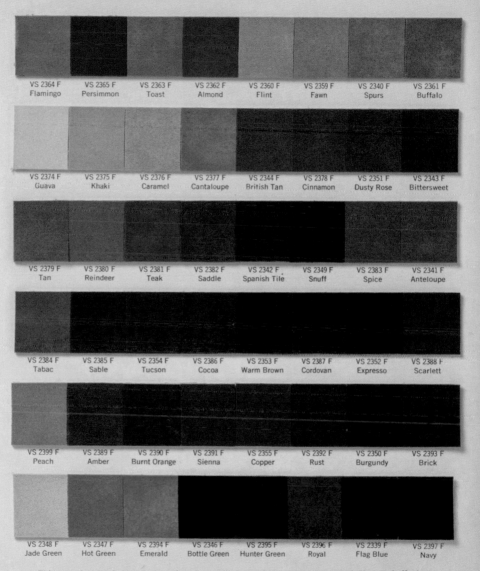

VS 2364 F Flamingo	VS 2365 F Persimmon	VS 2363 F Toast	VS 2362 F Almond	VS 2360 F Flint	VS 2359 F Fawn	VS 2340 F Spurs	VS 2361 F Buffalo
VS 2374 F Guava	VS 2375 F Khaki	VS 2376 F Caramel	VS 2377 F Cantaloupe	VS 2344 F British Tan	VS 2378 F Cinnamon	VS 2351 F Dusty Rose	VS 2343 F Bittersweet
VS 2379 F Tan	VS 2380 F Reindeer	VS 2381 F Teak	VS 2382 F Saddle	VS 2342 F Spanish Tile	VS 2349 F Snuff	VS 2383 F Spice	VS 2341 F Anteloupe
VS 2384 F Tabac	VS 2385 F Sable	VS 2354 F Tucson	VS 2386 F Cocoa	VS 2353 F Warm Brown	VS 2387 F Cordovan	VS 2352 F Expresso	VS 2388 F Scarlett
VS 2399 F Peach	VS 2389 F Amber	VS 2390 F Burnt Orange	VS 2391 F Sienna	VS 2355 F Copper	VS 2392 F Rust	VS 2350 F Burgundy	VS 2393 F Brick
VS 2348 F Jade Green	VS 2347 F Hot Green	VS 2394 F Emerald	VS 2346 F Bottle Green	VS 2395 F Hunter Green	VS 2396 F Royal	VS 2339 F Flag Blue	VS 2397 F Navy

This new vinyl fabric has all the unique features of Genuine Suede creating variable panel effects.

LARGE SAMPLES UPON REQUEST

W-G VINYLS INC. • 132 West 21st Street   New York, N.Y. 10011 • (212) 255-3300

DIAMONDHEAD SUEDE

Vinyl Wall & Upholstery Fabric

53-54 Inches Wide

WOLF-GORDON MINI-SPEC	ASTM E84 (Tunnel Test) RATING	
TOTAL WEIGHT: 30 OZ. LIN. YARD	FLAME SPREAD	20
FABRIC: POLYESTER-COTTON	FUEL CONTRIBUTED	15
ELASTIC BACKED	SMOKE DEVELOPED	25

DS 6250 F   CONVERT

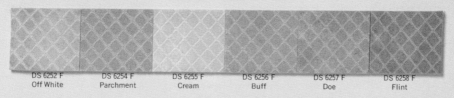

DS 6252 F	DS 6254 F	DS 6255 F	DS 6256 F	DS 6257 F	DS 6258 F
Off White	Parchment	Cream	Buff	Doe	Flint

DS 6251 F	DS 6259 F	DS 6250 F	DS 6260 F	DS 6261 F	DS 6262 F
Rattan	Mesh	Convert	Fawn	Camel	Beige

This new vinyl fabric has all the unique features of Genuine Suede creating variable panel effects.

LARGE SAMPLES UPON REQUEST

W-G VINYLS INC. • 132 West 21st Street   New York, N.Y. 10011 • (212) 255-3300

KORDA SUEDE
Vinyl Wall & Upholstery Fabric
52-54 Inches Wide

WOLF-GORDON MINI-SPEC	ASTM E84 (Tunnel Test) RATING	
TOTAL WEIGHT 32 OZ. LIN. YARD	FLAME SPREAD	20
FABRIC: SHEETING	FUEL CONTRIBUTED	10
	SMOKE DEVELOPED	35

KS 611 F   FLINT

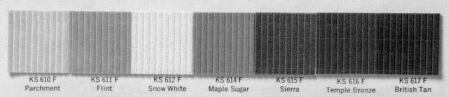

KS 610 F	KS 611 F	KS 612 F	KS 614 F	KS 615 F	KS 616 F	KS 617 F
Parchment	Flint	Snow White	Maple Sugar	Sierra	Temple Bronze	British Tan

KS 618 F	KS 619 F	KS 620 F	KS 621 F	KS 622 F	KS 623 F	KS 624 F
Burnished Gold	Spice	Rust	Amigo	Milk Chocolate	Tucson	Spanish Tile

KS 625 F	KS 626 F	KS 627 F	KS 628 F	KS 629 F	KS 630 F	KS 631 F
Maraschino	Jonquil	Klondike Gold	Old Gold	Gold Coin	Warm Brown	Dark Brown

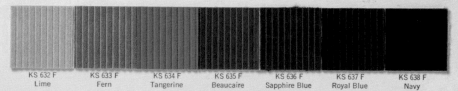

KS 632 F	KS 633 F	KS 634 F	KS 635 F	KS 636 F	KS 637 F	KS 638 F
Lime	Fern	Tangerine	Beaucaire	Sapphire Blue	Royal Blue	Navy

WOLF-GORDON VINYL FABRICS

W-G VINYLS INC. • 132 West 21st Street New York, N.Y. 10011 • (212) 255-3300

Textured Wallcoverings

WIDTH — 36 Inches   *100% Abaca Plant*
LENGTH — Two Rolls Per Bolt - 4 Yds. Per Roll

FIRE CLASSIFICATION
ASTM E84 (Tunnel Test)
FLAME SPREAD	25
FUEL CONTRIBUTED	0
SMOKE DEVELOPED	0

2318 E *100 A*	2319 E *Disc*	2320 E *100%A*	2321 E *Disc*
Jutewood	Drapewood	Maisewood	Silkwood

2322 E *100%A*	2323 E *100%A*	2324 E *100%A*	2325 E *100%A*
Sandwood	Roughwood	Lacewood	Aztecawood

2326 E *100%A*	2327 E *100% A*	Incawood *100%A*
Wovenwood	Windwood	2328 E

WOLF-GORDON TEXTURED WALLCOVERINGS   LARGE SAMPLES UPON REQUEST

W-G VINYLS, INC. • 132 West 21st Street New York, N.Y. 10011 • (212) 255-3300

Cotton

Wallcovering and Upholstery Fabric

WIDTH — 54 Inches
LENGTH — Sold by the Yard.

100% Cotton

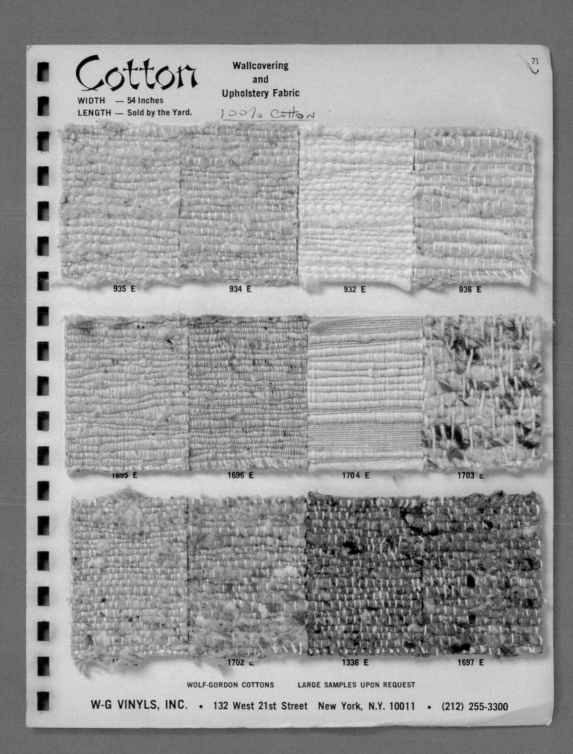

935 E	934 E	932 E	936 E
1695 E	1696 E	1704 E	1703 E
1702 E	1336 E	1697 E	

WOLF-GORDON COTTONS   LARGE SAMPLES UPON REQUEST

W-G VINYLS, INC. • 132 West 21st Street New York, N.Y. 10011 • (212) 255-3300

Linen

Paperbacked
For Wallcovering

WIDTH — 24 Inches
LENGTH — 6 Yards to the Roll - Sold in Double Rolls

FIRE CLASSIFICATION	
ASTM E84 (Tunnel Test)	
FLAME SPREAD	10
FUEL CONTRIBUTED	10
SMOKE DEVELOPED	0

1489 E   100% Linen

1302 E   95% Linen 5% Rayon

1486 E   100% Linen

1487 E   100% Linen

1488 E   100% Linen

1307 E   100% Linen

W-G VINYLS, INC.   •   132 West 21st Street   New York, N.Y. 10011   •   (212) 255-3300

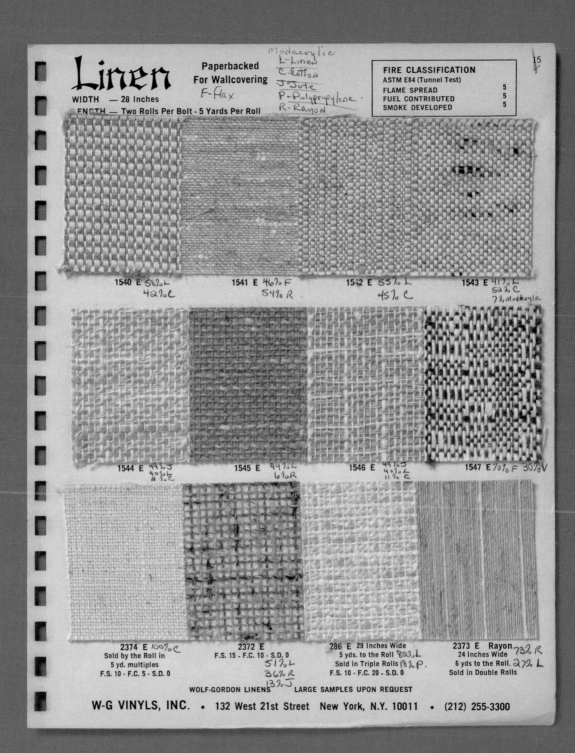

Linen

Paperbacked
For Wallcovering

Modacrylic
L-Linen
C-Cotton
J-Jute
F-Flax
P-Polypropylene
R-Rayon

WIDTH — 28 Inches

LENGTH — Two Rolls Per Bolt - 5 Yards Per Roll

FIRE CLASSIFICATION
ASTM E84 (Tunnel Test)
FLAME SPREAD   5
FUEL CONTRIBUTED   5
SMOKE DEVELOPED   5

1540 E 58%L
42%C

1541 E 46%F
54%R

1542 E 55%L
45%C

1543 E 41%L
52%C
7%modacrylic

1544 E 44%J
41%L

1545 E 94%L
6%R

1546 E 44%J
40%L
11%C

1547 E 70%F 30%V

2374 E 100%C
Sold by the Roll in
5 yd. multiples
F.S. 10 - F.C. 5 - S.D. 0

2372 E
F.S. 15 - F.C. 10 - S.D. 0
51%L
36%R
13%J

286 E 29 Inches Wide
5 yds. to the Roll 80%L
Sold in Triple Rolls 18%P.
F.S. 10 - F.C. 20 - S.D. 0

2373 E Rayon 73%R
24 Inches Wide
6 yds. to the Roll. 27%L
Sold in Double Rolls

WOLF-GORDON LINENS LARGE SAMPLES UPON REQUEST

W-G VINYLS, INC. • 132 West 21st Street New York, N.Y. 10011 • (212) 255-3300

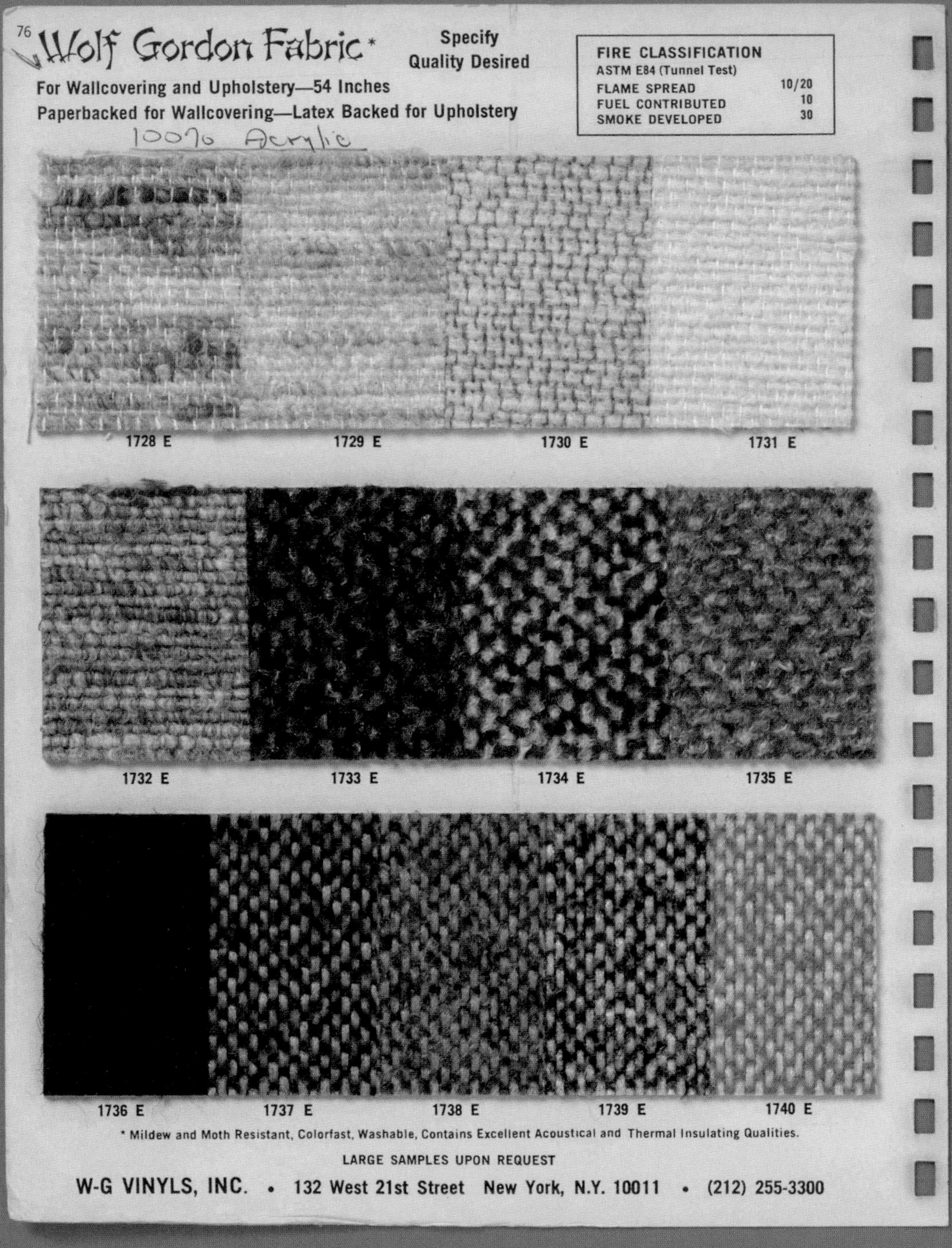

76 **Wolf Gordon Fabric** *

Specify Quality Desired

For Wallcovering and Upholstery—54 Inches
Paperbacked for Wallcovering—Latex Backed for Upholstery

100% Acrylic

FIRE CLASSIFICATION	
ASTM E84 (Tunnel Test)	
FLAME SPREAD	10/20
FUEL CONTRIBUTED	10
SMOKE DEVELOPED	30

1728 E   1729 E   1730 E   1731 E

1732 E   1733 E   1734 E   1735 E

1736 E   1737 E   1738 E   1739 E   1740 E

* Mildew and Moth Resistant, Colorfast, Washable, Contains Excellent Acoustical and Thermal Insulating Qualities.

LARGE SAMPLES UPON REQUEST

W-G VINYLS, INC. • 132 West 21st Street New York, N.Y. 10011 • (212) 255-3300

Bold Wool Stripes

WIDTH - 19.5 Inches Wide.
LENGTH - Sold By The Yard In 6 Yd. Multiples. _100% Wool_
Paperbacked In Continuous Yardage.

FIRE CLASSIFICATION
ASTM E 84 (Tunnel Test)

FLAME SPREAD	20
FUEL CONTRIBUTED	5
SMOKE DEVELOPED	35

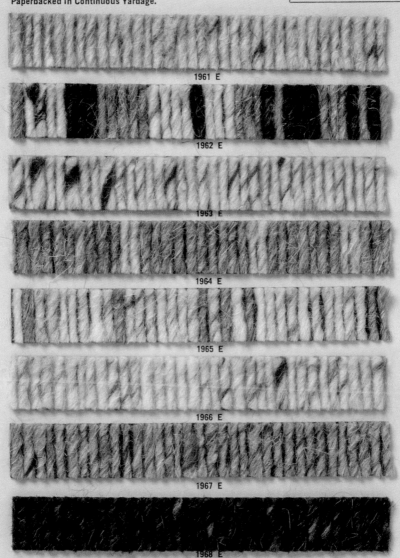

1961 E

1962 E

1963 E

1964 E

1965 E

1966 E

1967 E

1968 E

LARGE SAMPLES UPON REQUEST

W-G VINYLS, INC. • 132 West 21st Street   New York, N.Y. 10011 • (212) 255-3300

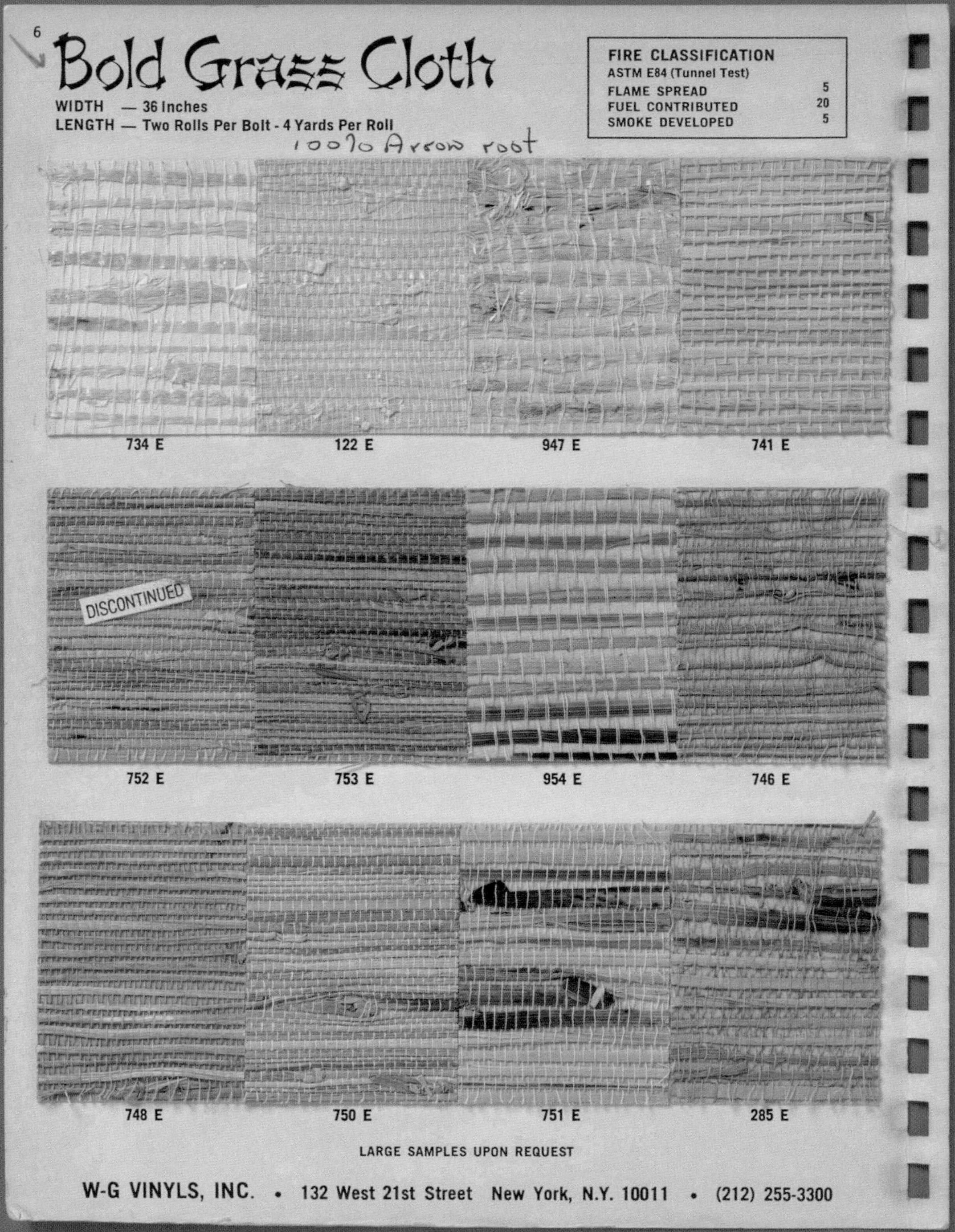

Bold Grass Cloth

WIDTH — 36 Inches
LENGTH — Two Rolls Per Bolt - 4 Yards Per Roll

100% Arrow root

FIRE CLASSIFICATION	
ASTM E84 (Tunnel Test)	
FLAME SPREAD	5
FUEL CONTRIBUTED	20
SMOKE DEVELOPED	5

734 E	122 E	947 E	741 E

DISCONTINUED

752 E	753 E	954 E	746 E

748 E	750 E	751 E	285 E

LARGE SAMPLES UPON REQUEST

W-G VINYLS, INC. • 132 West 21st Street New York, N.Y. 10011 • (212) 255-3300

Grass Cloth

WIDTH — 36 Inches
LENGTH — Three Rolls Per Bolt - 4 Yds. Per Roll 100% Arrowroot

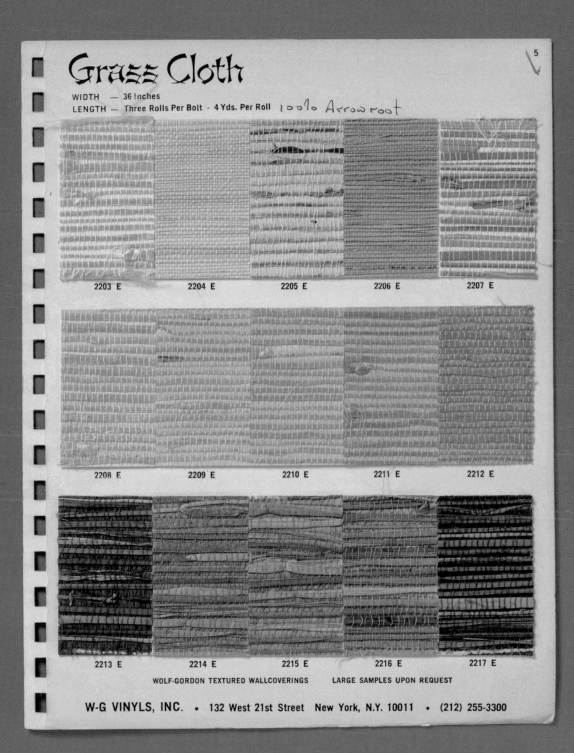

2203 E	2204 E	2205 E	2206 E	2207 E
2208 E	2209 E	2210 E	2211 E	2212 E
2213 E	2214 E	2215 E	2216 E	2217 E

WOLF-GORDON TEXTURED WALLCOVERINGS   LARGE SAMPLES UPON REQUEST

W-G VINYLS, INC. • 132 West 21st Street New York, N.Y. 10011 • (212) 255-3300

33

LA MANCHA CORK

Natural Cork Chip on Fabric

36 Inches Wide

WOLF-GORDON MINI-SPEC	
ASTM E84 (Tunnel Test) RATING	
FLAME SPREAD	3
FUEL CONTRIBUTED	0
SMOKE DEVELOPED	0

LA MANCHA - LA 9155 F   ANTIQUE TOAST

LA 9163 F	LA 9168 F	LA 9157 F	LA 9156 F	LA 9151 F	LA 9152 F	LA 9153 F
Chalk White	Snow	White	Sand	Natural	Toast	Charcoal

CORTEZ CORK

Natural Cork Chip on Fabric

36-37 Inches Wide

WOLF-GORDON MINI-SPEC	
ASTM E84 (Tunnel Test) RATING	
FLAME SPREAD	3
FUEL CONTRIBUTED	0
SMOKE DEVELOPED	0

CTZ 8115 F	CTZ 8111 F	CTZ 8112 F	CTZ 8113 F	CTZ 8114 F
Chalk White	Natural	Sand	Toast	Charcoal

LARGE SAMPLES UPON REQUEST

W-G VINYLS INC. • 132 West 21st Street New York, N.Y. 10011 • (212) 255-3300

CORTICIERA
VIN-A-TEX — Natural Cork on Fabric
Decorative Wall Cork — 49 Inches Wide

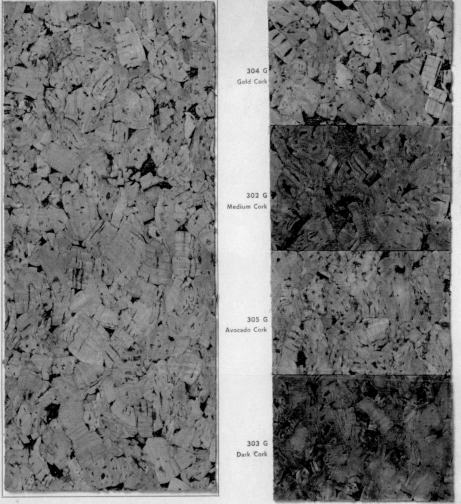

304 G
Gold Cork

302 G
Medium Cork

305 G
Avocado Cork

303 G
Dark Cork

301 G NATURAL CORK

CORTICIERA is Composed of Rugged Chunks of Natural Cork Fused to a Heavy Fabric Backing.
Its Unique Cellular Structure Provides Accoustical and Insulation Values.

WOLF-GORDON VINYL FABRICS • 132 West 21st Street   New York, N.Y. 10011 • 212-255-3300

RENO
Wall Carpet
48 Inches Wide

ACOUSTICAL RATING: NRC .20-.30

WOLF-GORDON MINI-SPEC	
TOTAL WEIGHT: 27 OZ. LIN YARD	
FABRIC: Acoustical Fade Resistant	
Poly-propylene Fiber Facing	
BACKING: FUSED BONDING	

ASTM E84 (Tunnel Test) RATING	
FLAME SPREAD	25
FUEL CONTRIBUTED	20
SMOKE DEVELOPED	20

R 8930 F   CHESTNUT

R 8931 F	R 8932 F	R 8933 F	R 8934 F	R 8935 F	R 8936 F
Oyster	Natural	Beige	Pewter	Slate Grey	Amber

R 8937 F	R 8938 F	R 8939 F	R 8940 F	R 8941 F	R 8942 F
Clay	Mahogany	Oak Brown	Cranberry	Terra Cotta	Blue

LARGE SAMPLES UPON REQUEST
WOLF-GORDON VINYL FABRICS

W-G VINYLS INC.   •   132 West 21st Street   New York, N.Y. 10011   •   (212) 255-3300

CANBERRA WOOL

Wall & Upholstery Fabric

54 Inches Wide — Acrylic Backed
Du Pont Zepel® Stain Tested
Resists Oily & Greasy Stains — Sheds Water

WOLF-GORDON MINI-SPEC		ASTM E84 (Tunnel Test) RATING	
TOTAL WEIGHT:	21 OZ. LIN. YARD	FLAME SPREAD	15
FABRIC:	80% WOOL - 20% NYLON	FUEL CONTRIBUTED	5
		SMOKE DEVELOPED	0

CB 5842 F   BEIGE

CB 5841 F	CB 5842 F	CB 5843 F	CB 5844 F	CB 5845 F	CB 5846 F	CB 5847 F
Putty	Beige	Camel	Doeskin	Moonstone	Bronze	Brown

CB 5848 F	CB 5849 F	CB 5850 F	CB 5851 F	CB 5852 F	CB 5853 F	CB 5854 F
Pagoda	Red	Bordeau	Lemon	Antique	Jade	Moss

CB 5840 F	CB 5855 F	CB 5856 F	CB 5858 F	CB 5859 F	CB 5860 F	CB 5861 F
Bamboo	Apricot	Clay	Monaco	Royal	Blue	Black

W-G VINYLS INC. • 132 West 21st Street   New York, N.Y. 10011 • (212) 255-3300

AQUARIUS
VIN-A-TEX – Vinyl Wall Fabric
54 Inches Wide

WOLF - GORDON MINI - SPEC	ASTM E84 [TUNNEL TEST] RATING	
EXCEEDS FED. SPEC. CCCW 408A – TYPE II	FLAME SPREAD	15
TOTAL WEIGHT – 26 OZ. LIN. YARD	FUEL CONTRIBUTED	0
FABRIC – OSNABURG	SMOKE DEVELOPED	15

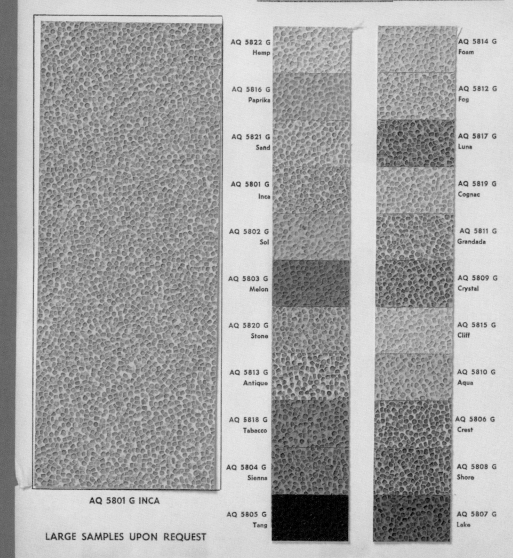

AQ 5801 G INCA

AQ 5822 G Hemp

AQ 5816 G Paprika

AQ 5821 G Sand

AQ 5801 G Inca

AQ 5802 G Sol

AQ 5803 G Melon

AQ 5820 G Stone

AQ 5813 G Antique

AQ 5818 G Tabacco

AQ 5804 G Sienna

AQ 5805 G Tang

AQ 5814 G Foam

AQ 5812 G Fog

AQ 5817 G Luna

AQ 5819 G Cognac

AQ 5811 G Grandada

AQ 5809 G Crystal

AQ 5815 G Cliff

AQ 5810 G Aqua

AQ 5806 G Crest

AQ 5808 G Shore

AQ 5807 G Lake

LARGE SAMPLES UPON REQUEST

WOLF - GORDON VINYL FABRICS • 132 West 21st Street   New York, N. Y. 10011 • 212 – 255 – 3300

MERCURY

VIN-A-TEX – Vinyl Wall Fabric – 54 Inches Wide
Available in 43 Designer Colors

MR 7223 G Red Gold	MR 7236 G Tangerine	MR 7235 G Navy Blue
MR 7222 G Emerald	MR 7237 G Flamingo	MR 7229 G Lavender
MR 7207 G Avocado	MR 7233 G Flame	MR 7226 G Majestic
MR 7209 G Peridot	MR 7220 G Tulip	MR 7242 G Periwinkle
MR 7230 G Kelly	MR 7202 G Cerulean Blue	MR 7241 G Gunmetal
MR 7243 G Bright Green	MR 7213 G Teal	MR 7232 G Desert Brown
MR 7228 G Orange Peel	MR 7211 G Manganese	MR 7204 G Dark Bronze
MR 7214 G Amber Glow	MR 7218 G Deep Blue	MR 7225 G Black

LARGE SAMPLES UPON REQUEST

WOLF-GORDON VINYL FABRICS • 132 West 21st Street   New York, N. Y. 10011 • 212 – 255 - 3300

PONDEROSA

Vinyl Wall Fabric

53-54 Inches Wide

WOLF-GORDON MINI - SPEC	ASTM E84 (Tunnel Test) RATING	
EXCEEDS FED. SPEC. CCCW 408A - TYPE II	FLAME SPREAD	15
TOTAL WEIGHT: 36 OZ. LIN. YARD	FUEL CONTRIBUTED	0
FABRIC: OSNABURG	SMOKE DEVELOPED	30

PSA 4470 F   SMOKE HOUSE

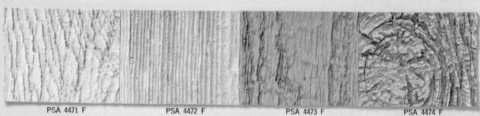

PSA 4471 F	PSA 4472 F	PSA 4473 F	PSA 4474 F
Beech	Poplar	Hickory	Barnboard

PSA 4475 F	PSA 4476 F	PSA 4477 F	PSA 4478 F
Buckeye	Conestoga	Tidewater	Charwood

LARGE SAMPLES UPON REQUEST

W-G VINYLS INC.   •   132 West 21st Street   New York, N.Y. 10011   •   (212) 255-3300

VALDEZ STRIPE

Vinyl Wall Fabric

53-54 Inches Wide

WOLF-GORDON MINI-SPEC	ASTM E84 (Tunnel Test) RATING	
EXCEEDS FED. SPEC. CCCW 408A - TYPE I	FLAME SPREAD	15
TOTAL WEIGHT: 14/15 OZ. LIN. YARD	FUEL CONTRIBUTED	0
FABRIC: SHEETING	SMOKE DEVELOPED	10

VAS 166 F   FRAPPE

VAS 167 F   EXPRESSO

VAS 168 F   SUDAN IVORY

VAS 169 F   BLUE PRINT

VAS 170 F   MOSQUE

VAS 171 F   SORRENTO

VAS 172 F   HIGH TIDE

VAS 173 F   CARAVAN

VAS 174 F   DELTA

LARGE SAMPLES UPON REQUEST   WOLF-GORDON VINYL FABRICS

W-G VINYLS INC.   •   132 West 21st Street   New York, N.Y. 10011   •   (212) 255-3300

MULTITONE

Vinyl Wall Fabric
53-54 Inches Wide

WOLF-GORDON MINI-SPEC	ASTM E84 (Tunnel Test) RATING	
EXCEEDS FED. SPEC. CCCW 408A TYPE II	FLAME SPREAD	5-15
TOTAL WEIGHT: 21 OZ. LIN. YARD	SMOKE DEVELOPED	15-20
FABRIC: OSNABURG		

MLT 3-282 F   NEUTRAL

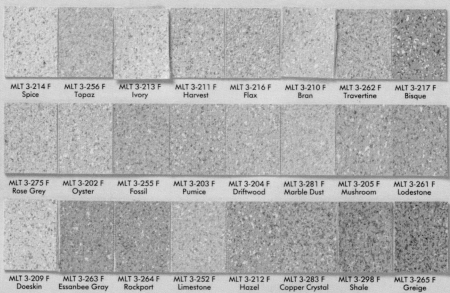

MLT 3-214 F Spice	MLT 3-256 F Topaz	MLT 3-213 F Ivory	MLT 3-211 F Harvest	MLT 3-216 F Flax	MLT 3-210 F Bran	MLT 3-262 F Travertine	MLT 3-217 F Bisque
MLT 3-275 F Rose Grey	MLT 3-202 F Oyster	MLT 3-255 F Fossil	MLT 3-203 F Pumice	MLT 3-204 F Driftwood	MLT 3-281 F Marble Dust	MLT 3-205 F Mushroom	MLT 3-261 F Lodestone
MLT 3-209 F Doeskin	MLT 3-263 F Essanbee Gray	MLT 3-264 F Rockport	MLT 3-252 F Limestone	MLT 3-212 F Hazel	MLT 3-283 F Copper Crystal	MLT 3-298 F Shale	MLT 3-265 F Greige

LARGE SAMPLES UPON REQUEST
WOLF-GORDON INC.
33-00 47th Avenue ● Long Island City, N.Y. 11101 ● (718) 361-6611

MULTITONE — 74 Standard Stock Colors

MLT 3-251 F Sand	MLT 3-224 F Autumn	MLT 3-276 F Talcum	MLT 3-270 F Lavender Grey	MLT 3-267 F Jasper Tint	MLT 3-208 F Earth	MLT 3-299 F Cinder	MLT 3-269 F Serpentine
MLT 3-218 F Cameo	MLT 3-220 F Blush	MLT 3-219 F Pink Sand	MLT 3-277 F Quartz	MLT 3-222 F Tawny	MLT 3-221 F Apache	MLT 3-278 F Strata Pink	MLT 3-279 F Rosetone
MLT 3-226 F Thistle	MLT 3-225 F Orchid	MLT 3-223 F Cedar	MLT 3-273 F Amethyst	MLT 3-227 F Desire	MLT 3-271 F Opal	MLT 3-272 F Pink Calcite	MLT 3-300 F Emberglow
MLT 3-291 F Granite	MLT 3-290 F Frost	MLT 3-293 F Bluestone	MLT 3-232 F Blue Snow	MLT 3-229 F Blue Pine	MLT 3-228 F Moonstone	MLT 3-294 F Malachite	MLT 3-296 F Azurite
MLT 3-234 F Clamshell	MLT 3-295 F Silvermine	MLT 3-235 F Dawn	MLT 3-207 F Aspen	MLT 3-284 F Uranium	MLT 3-236 F Pewter	MLT 3-206 F Dusty	MLT 3-292 F Blue Tourmaline
MLT 3-215 F Putty	MLT 3-230 F Zephyr	MLT 3-289 F Jade Grey	MLT 3-231 F Verde	MLT 3-287 F Emerald	MLT 3-201 F Cascade	MLT 3-233 F Sumara	MLT 3-286 F Bornite	MLT 3-297 F Ash

LARGE SAMPLES UPON REQUEST
WOLF-GORDON INC.
33-00 47th Avenue • Long Island City, N.Y. 11101 • (718) 361-6611

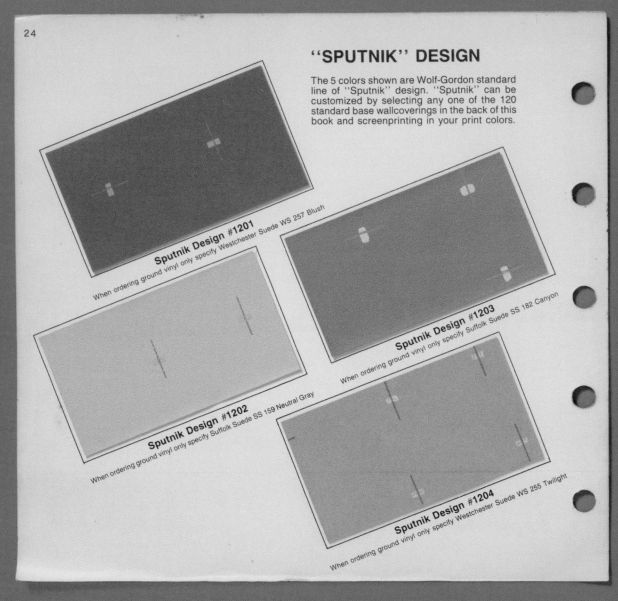

"SPUTNIK" DESIGN

The 5 colors shown are Wolf-Gordon standard line of "Sputnik" design. "Sputnik" can be customized by selecting any one of the 120 standard base wallcoverings in the back of this book and screenprinting in your print colors.

Sputnik Design #1201
When ordering ground vinyl only specify Westchester Suede WS 257 Blush

Sputnik Design #1203
When ordering ground vinyl only specify Suffolk Suede SS 182 Canyon

Sputnik Design #1202
When ordering ground vinyl only specify Suffolk Suede SS 159 Neutral Gray

Sputnik Design #1204
When ordering ground vinyl only specify Westchester Suede WS 255 Twilight

Designed by Patty Madden

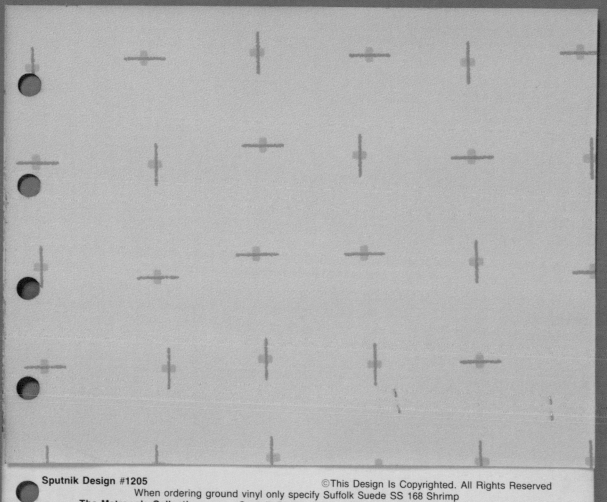

Sputnik Design #1205

©This Design Is Copyrighted. All Rights Reserved

When ordering ground vinyl only specify Suffolk Suede SS 168 Shrimp

The Metropole Collection — Sputnik Design Sample Shown Is Printed On Suffolk Suede.

120 Additional Wallcovering Ground Colors Are Shown In The Back Of The Book.

Width Of Ground Vinyl - 53/54 Inches Wide • Width Of Screen - 51 Inches • Design Repeat — 9-3/4 Inches

WOLF-GORDON INC. 132 West 21st Street • New York, N.Y. 10011 • (212) 255-3300

Designed by Patty Madden

45

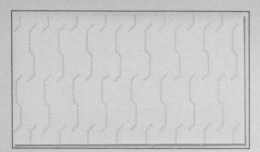

Fences Design #801

When ordering ground vinyl only specify Suffolk Suede SS 167 Waxen

"FENCES" DESIGN

The Metropole Collection is your opportunity to create your own distinctive wallcovering.

1 . Select the design of your choice from the 15 original designs shown.
2 . Select your vinyl ground from the 120 shown in the back of the book.
3 . Select your own print colors.
4 . In addition, specify any of the grounds for areas without screenprinting.

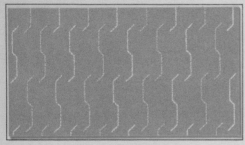

Fences Design #802

When ordering ground vinyl only specify Westchester Suede WS 255 Twilight

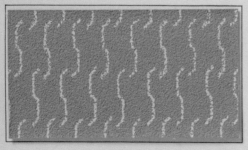

Fences Design #803

When ordering ground vinyl only specify Nassau Stucco NS 369 Mauve

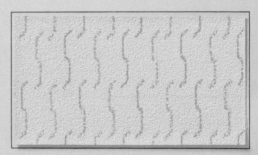

Fences Design #804

When ordering ground vinyl only specify Nassau Stucco NS 333 Duck

Designed by Patty Madden

Fences Design #805   ©This Design Is Copyrighted. All Rights Reserved
When ordering ground vinyl only specify Westchester Suede WS 260 Pebble
The Metropole Collection   —   Fences Design Sample Shown Is Printed On Westchester Suede.
120 Additional Wallcovering Ground Colors Are Shown In The Back Of The Book.
Width Of Ground Vinyl - 53/54 Inches Wide • Width Of Screen - 50-1/2 Inches • Design Repeat — 2 Inches

WOLF-GORDON INC. 132 West 21st Street • New York, N.Y. 10011 • (212) 255-3300

Designed by Patty Madden

MAYAN STUCCO

Vinyl Wall Fabric
53-54 Inches Wide

WOLF-GORDON MINI-SPEC	ASTM E84 (Tunnel Test) RATING	
EXCEEDS FED. SPEC. CCCW 408A TYPE II	FLAME SPREAD	5-15
TOTAL WEIGHT: 20-21 OZ. LIN. YARD	SMOKE DEVELOPED	25 max.
FABRIC: OSNABURG		

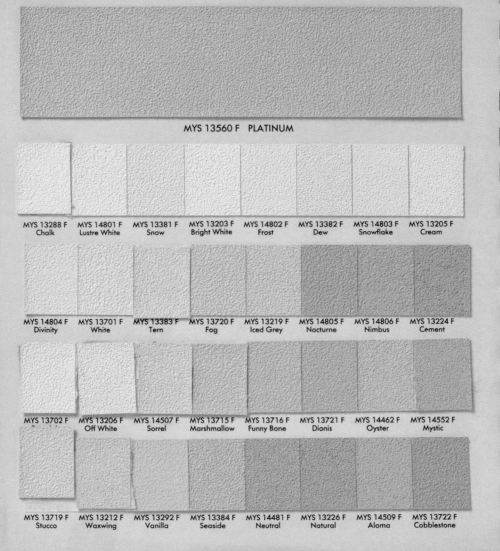

MYS 13560 F PLATINUM

MYS 13288 F	MYS 14801 F	MYS 13381 F	MYS 13203 F	MYS 14802 F	MYS 13382 F	MYS 14803 F	MYS 13205 F
Chalk	Lustre White	Snow	Bright White	Frost	Dew	Snowflake	Cream

MYS 14804 F	MYS 13701 F	MYS 13383 F	MYS 13720 F	MYS 13219 F	MYS 14805 F	MYS 14806 F	MYS 13224 F
Divinity	White	Tern	Fog	Iced Grey	Nocturne	Nimbus	Cement

MYS 13702 F	MYS 13206 F	MYS 14507 F	MYS 13715 F	MYS 13716 F	MYS 13721 F	MYS 14462 F	MYS 14552 F
	Off White	Sorrel	Marshmallow	Funny Bone	Dionis	Oyster	Mystic

MYS 13719 F	MYS 13212 F	MYS 13292 F	MYS 13384 F	MYS 14481 F	MYS 13226 F	MYS 14509 F	MYS 13722 F
Stucco	Waxwing	Vanilla	Seaside	Neutral	Natural	Aloma	Cobblestone

LARGE SAMPLES UPON REQUEST
WOLF-GORDON INC.
33-00 47th Avenue ● Long Island City, N.Y. 11101 ● (718) 361-6611

PATTERN PALETTE

Over our history, the arc of Wolf-Gordon's product lines has paralleled trends in commercial interior design. When Mel Wolf and Bernie Gordon founded the company in 1967, our products were "open line," which meant that other distributors could present the same products to the same customers. We competed only on price.

By the 1990s, it had become clear that exclusive products were the most exciting—and competitive—path forward. David Gordon began to work with freelance wallcovering stylists and mills' in-house design studios on unique Wolf-Gordon patterning. While these collections began to set us apart, it was the introduction in 2001 of Linework by Laurinda Spear that proved seminal. Spear's work redefined the role that walls could play in commercial interiors. This collaboration was the first of many with concept-driven designers nationally and internationally.

At the same time, our in-house team, Wolf-Gordon Design Studio, was establishing itself as a talented and versatile creator of branded products. Custom wallcovering design also increased as our business in the hospitality sector grew and as customers became more interested in designing signature, site-specific interiors.

Today, Wolf-Gordon Design Studio develops wallcovering, upholstery, and drapery textiles alone and in concert with creative professionals from diverse design disciplines. The mix of products, which covers what is trending in contract interiors and also offers innovative concepts from outside the industry, reinforces our position as a design leader.

Open Line/Exclusive Line

In our early years, we presented products to our customers in various sample books. Although the products were not exclusive to Wolf-Gordon, the sample books were compiled with care, flair, and an eye to trends. The wallcovering lines developed by David Gordon in the mid-1990s were a first step toward what has become our signature, uniquely colored and patterned wallcoverings. Translations and Circa, released in 1996 and 1997, featured designs that were simple and subtle, with a range of colorways tailored to the conservative interiors of the decade.

Cyber (from Circa Collection)

Linework

Laurinda Spear's bold motifs and saturated color palettes contributed to an awakening of interest in dramatic wall patterning. Extensively published and discussed, her designs set a high bar for innovation and differentiation. Linework remains an important collection for Wolf-Gordon; the now classic Bamboo design is one of the company's all-time best-selling patterns. The collection as a whole was named to the *New York Times Magazine*'s "A List" in 2001.

Advertisements, designed by 2x4, for Palmrail, Bamboo, Wave, designed by Laurinda Spear

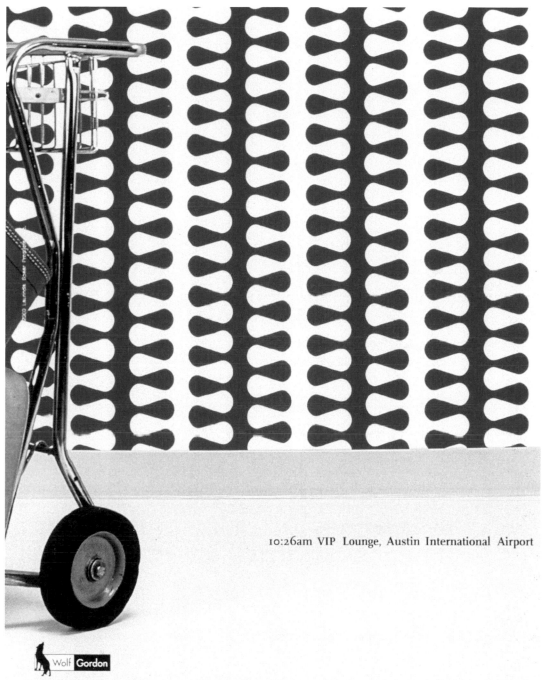

10:26am VIP Lounge, Austin International Airport

Digital Nature

Prolific designer Karim Rashid turned his attention to wallcoverings with the Digital Nature collection of 2002. His graceful manipulations of computer-generated drawings transformed topographic, zoomorphic, and skeletal geometries into futuristic excavations. Rashid's use of fluorescent and iridescent inks was a first for commercial wallcoverings.

Replicant, designed by Karim Rashid

Flexuous, designed by Karim Rashid

Touch

Dutch designer Petra Blaisse's seven-pattern Touch collection of 2003 reveals both the impact of the photographic process on design and the resurgence of materiality. Blaisse enlarged photos of materials—crocheted sheer fabric, stitched felt, wool rope, human hair, and fur—to heroic proportions. The hyperrealistic designs create an illusion of dimensionality on a flat surface and explore the relationship between interior space and the walls that contain that space.

Source materials for Touch, Knitte #1, designed by Petra Blaisse

Kit of Parts

In 2008, Wolf-Gordon collaborated with Gensler on an innovative and flexible set of wallcoverings. Composed in two series, City and Nature, Kit of Parts enabled designers to assemble custom wallcovering by juxtaposing patterns and colors, mixing and matching forms, and positioning panels in a standard or reverse composition. With ten different colorways per pattern, Kit of Parts generated different designs without compromising a fluid effect.

Tree, Blossom (from Nature Series), designed in collaboration with Gensler

Surface Over Structure

In 2006, we conducted a seminar and design competition at the Harvard Graduate School of Design, teaching architecture students how to engineer patterning. Winners Corinne Ulmann and Isamu Kanda started with images of the play of light across their walls; the design, Light, is an uncanny re-creation of sunbeams and shadows. This trompe l'oeil wallcovering promotes natural depth and spatial qualities, sculpting spaces two-dimensionally.

Light, designed by Corinne Ulmann and Isamu Kanda

Transport, designed by Zac Culbreth

Independent Voices

Our collaborating designers are inspired by diverse and unpredictable themes. Calvin Tsao and Zack McKown explored the course of time and the effects of weathering in Passage. Kevin Walz used translucent inks to simulate the effect of paint seeping through a canvas in patterns of hand-drawn forms and painted textures. In Tall and Wide, Morgan Bajardi exercised her knowledge of visual perception, employing continuous line striation to create an illusion of taller or longer surfaces.

Flower, designed by Tsao & McKown

Birch, designed by Tsao & McKown

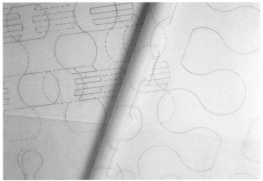

Nite, source materials for Overlay/Underlay, Marz, designed by Kevin Walz

Engineered Illusions dresses, Wide, designed by Morgan Bajardi

Grethe Sørensen Collection

Danish textile artist Grethe Sørensen works at the cutting edge of craft and technology. Three wallcovering patterns render what she calls "unfocused images of light," from photographs of busy, traffic-filled streets, into pixelated stripes, gradated dots, and soft stripes. The centerpiece of the collection is our first wool upholstery textile, Millions of Colors, in which Sørensen's signature "random weave" technique translates pools of light into luxurious fabric.

Blinds, designed by Grethe Sørensen

Millions of Colors, Codes, designed by Grethe Sørensen

Recollections

Industrial designers Constantin and Laurene Boym create witty, tongue-in-cheek products of great depth and sensitivity. For Wolf-Gordon, they celebrated in contract wallcoverings their memories of significant materials from their travels. Broadway is closest to home, a trompe l'oeil interpretation of a velvet theater curtain; Glasgow, a textural print, is based on the deconstruction of a traditional Scottish plaid; Jaipur evokes the handcrafts of India and includes "hidden" Hindu imagery; and Venice pays homage to the Venetian mosaics of architect Carlo Scarpa.

Venice, Glasgow, designed by Boym Partners

Tjep.Cubism

A cubic matrix was the starting point for Frank Tjepkema's patterns for upholstery, wallcoverings, and drapery fabrics. The Dutch designer, who works at such divergent scales as jewelry and public parks, deconstructed the cube from several different perspectives, including structural development, transformation, weathering, and the merging of his matrix with a traditional damask motif. We debuted Tjep.Cubism at the Spazio Rossana Orlandi in Milan in April 2015. This was the first time we launched a collection in an international venue.

Introduction of Tjep.Cubism in Milan, Metamorphosis, designed by Tjep.

Baroque, designed by Tjep.

Wolf-Gordon Design Studio

Our in-house creative team, Wolf-Gordon Design Studio, brings together individuals with expertise in fine art, pattern engineering, color forecasting, and textile and environmental design. Over a period of eight to ten months, the group shepherds products from concept through design development and color work and ultimately to manufacturing. In addition to work on in-house designs, the Studio is an essential contributor to all licensed design collections: the team works with our independent design partners, who are almost exclusively from outside the wallcovering industry, to make their concepts into viable products.

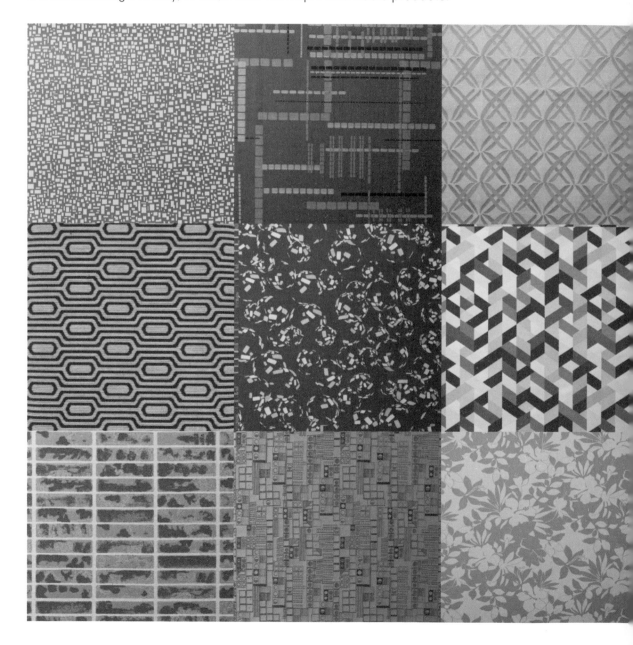

Digital at WG Customs Lab

Digital print technology has opened up great opportunities for unique wallcoverings in contract interiors, as it has for many other products. Digital printing provides increased flexibility for pattern complexity and infinite colors. WG Customs Lab helps interior designers create site-specific products based on all sorts of visual and conceptual themes, from photographic and illustrative origins to wayfinding, supergraphics, and branding scaled to the wall.

Break room, Tredway Lumsdaine & Doyle, Irvine, California, designed by Kardent Design

Mission Integration Center, John Glenn Research Center, NASA, Cleveland, Ohio, designed by Stantec

SLICE

Our first technology-focused Ad Sculpture, the thirty-foot-long SLICE, captured images of riders at the foot of the Merchandise Mart's first-to-second-floor escalator during NeoCon 2015. These images were processed through cameras embedded in the LED screen into increasingly abstracted forms, resulting in a grid of color fields. Our design partner, karlssonwilker, used these human-body-generated patterns in a compelling digital wallcovering named for the sculpture.

Image data captured by SLICE

SLICE digital print wallcovering, designed by karlssonwilker inc.

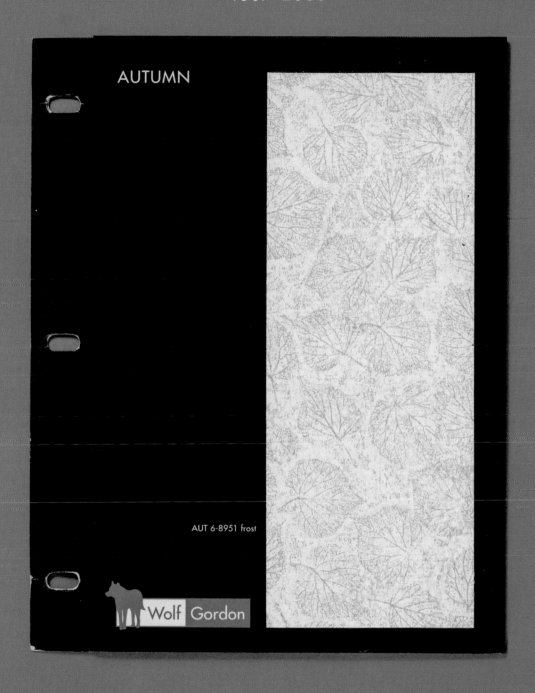

AUTUMN

AUT 6-8951 frost

Wolf Gordon

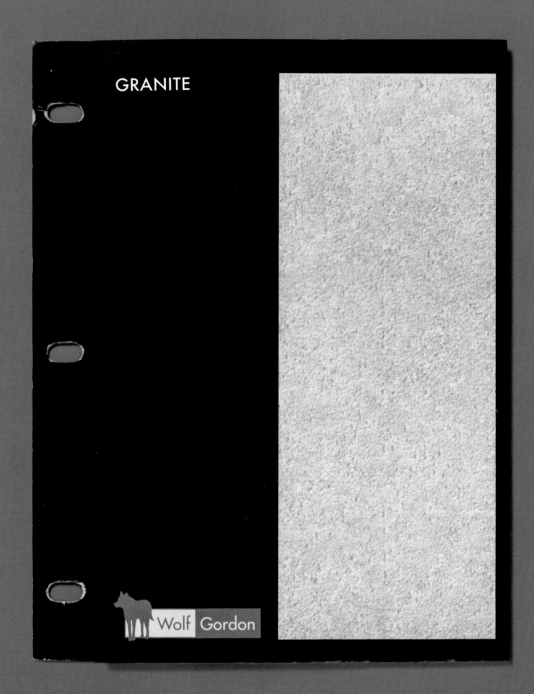

GRANITE

Wolf Gordon

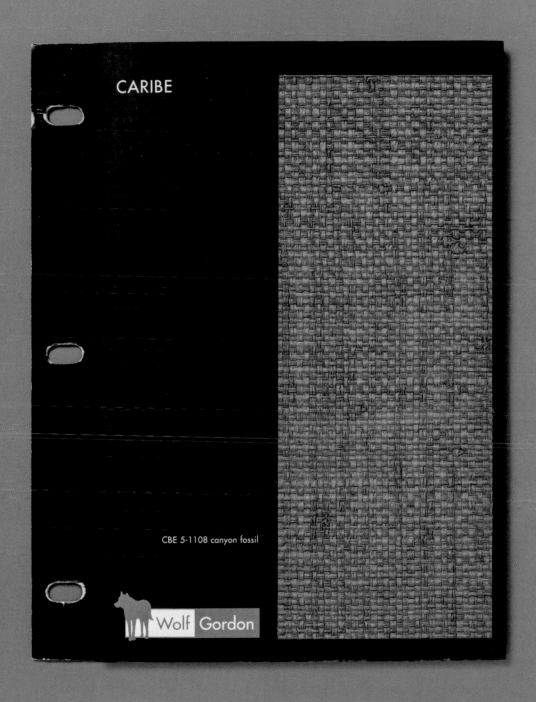

CARIBE

CBE 5-1108 canyon fossil

Wolf Gordon

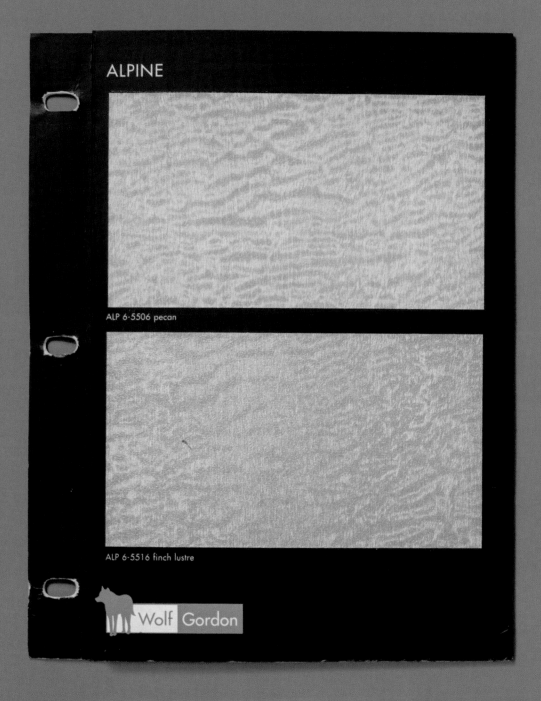

ALPINE

ALP 6-5506 pecan

ALP 6-5516 finch lustre

Wolf Gordon

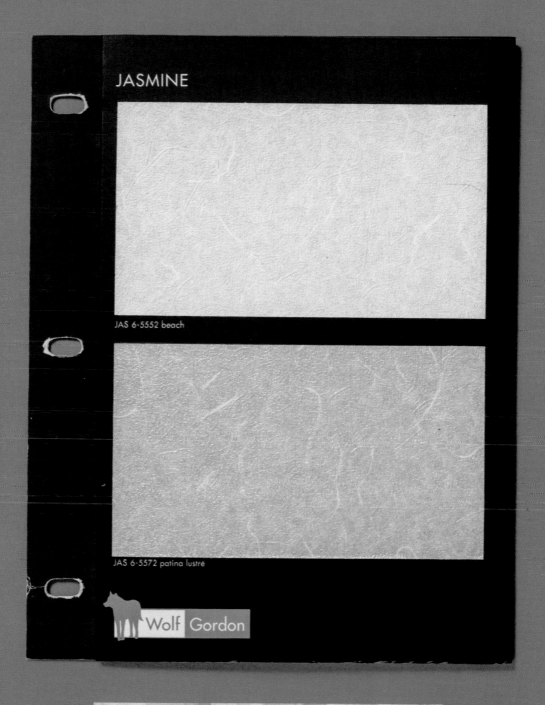

JASMINE

JAS 6·5552 beach

JAS 6·5572 patina lustré

Wolf Gordon

RAIN

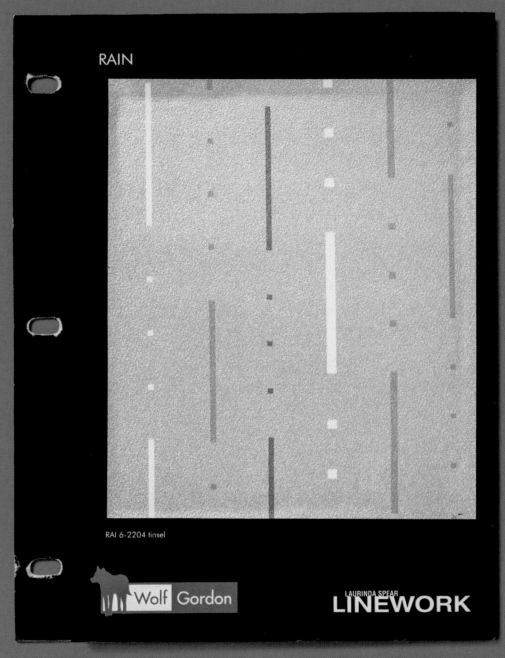

RAI 6-2204 tinsel

Wolf Gordon

LAURINDA SPEAR
LINEWORK

Designed by Laurinda Spear

PALMRAIL

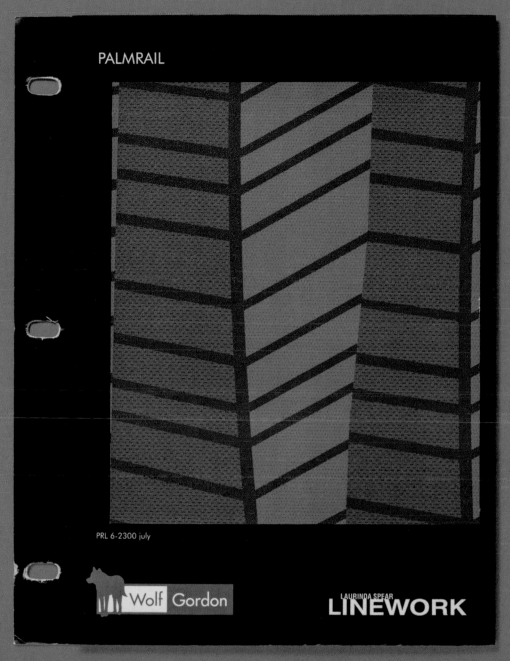

PRL 6-2300 july

Wolf Gordon

LAURINDA SPEAR
LINEWORK

Designed by Laurinda Spear

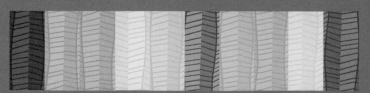

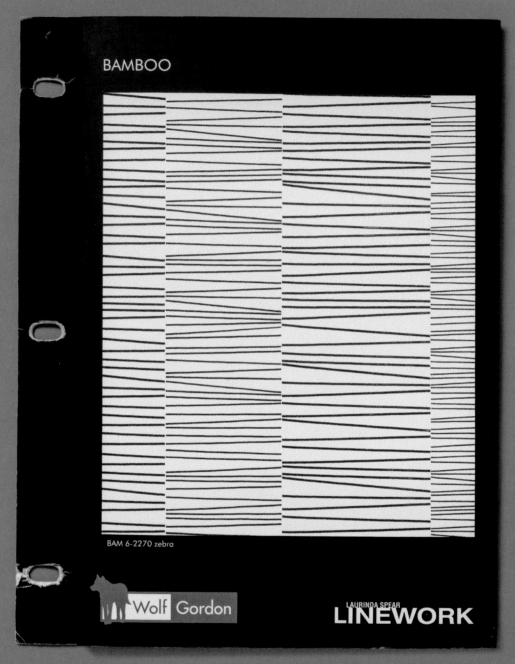

BAMBOO

BAM 6-2270 zebra

Wolf Gordon

LAURINDA SPEAR
LINEWORK

Designed by Laurinda Spear

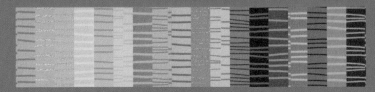

WAVE

WAV 6-2353 vence blue

Wolf Gordon

LAURINDA SPEAR
LINEWORK

Designed by Laurinda Spear

**Vinyl
Wallcovering**

**54" Contract Wallcovering
Type II**

Designed by Karim Rashid

Wolf-Gordon introduces
Digital Nature by Karim Rashid

FLEXUOUS · ROSETTA · REPLICANT · SPACE WARP · ZENITH

Exploring new ways to reference patterning found in Nature, Karim Rashid digitally generated these five designs and manipulated them to resemble multiple plant, animal, land and human anatomies, as well as forging new ground in two-dimensional pattern-making.

FLEXUOUS

Designed by Karim Rashid

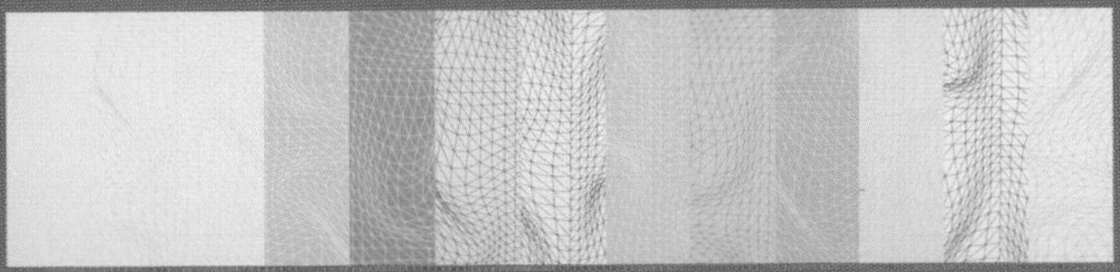

EASTERN MORSE

Eastern Morse was derived from textures found in nature, such as tree bark, rocks and hemp. Magnified and repeated, Weisberg transforms the source images into a visual shorthand. To recreate the individuality of patterns found in nature, Eastern Morse was meticulously hand drawn. The overall effect of the design is a deliberate lack of uniformity that stays true to its natural origins while adapting beautifully to traditional and transitional interiors.

DESIGNED BY CARLA WEISBERG

Wolf Gordon

Designed by Carla Weisberg

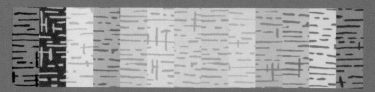

METEOR

Meteor was inspired by a favorite childhood toy: Pick-Up Sticks. The layering of colored lines when one first empties the container of sticks always delighted designer Kari Pei. With Meteor, walls can wear vibrant color and become activated, engaging one with the space. Meteor Stripe offers a reconfiguration of the color sticks into parallel order.

DESIGNED BY KARI PEI

Designed by Kari Pei

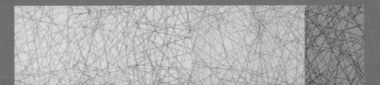

TOUCH
Wallcovering
by Petra Blaisse

CORD 2

Designed by Petra Blaisse

TOUCH
Wallcovering
by Petra Blaisse

CORD 1

Designed by Petra Blaisse

TOUCH
Wallcovering
by Petra Blaisse

FUR 1

Designed by Petra Blaisse

TAKING FORM

Our products are destined for interior spaces, so we spend a lot of time thinking in three dimensions. When it comes to presenting wallcoverings, textiles, and specialty coatings in a showroom or trade show environment, we use this perspective to reconsider traditional means of product display.

Permanent showrooms in New York, Chicago, and Los Angeles and transitory booths for trade shows present our stubbornly two-dimensional products to professionals and to the public. With the help of talented architects and designers, these spatial constructs showcase Wolf-Gordon products with attention to abundance, variety, and design intent.

Engagement is an ongoing pursuit in our creative department. Projects like the Exquisite Wink and Fun House booths seek a reciprocal experience between visitor and product. When customers reach out to touch a sample in our flagship showroom, or interact with a trompe l'oeil table at Dining by Design, the annual fundraiser for DIFFA (Design Industries Foundation Fighting AIDS), we have succeeded.

The Gift of Hope program is a special initiative in the interior design community. Through the program, created by Wolf-Gordon in 1992, specifiers can direct a percentage of sales revenues to DIFFA by ordering with a Gift of Hope number. In the twenty-plus years since the program's inception, Wolf-Gordon has been DIFFA's largest contributor, exceeding $1.6 million as of 2016.

New York Showroom

To coincide with the launch of our new identity and first ever website in 1998, Baratloo-Balch Architects designed a showroom for us in the D&D Building. The long narrow space features a flexible grid of more than five hundred picture frames on all four walls. When upholstery was added to the product line in 2012, we designed abstract, three-dimensional forms that fit within the same frames, generating an upholstered "topography" of textile sculptures interspersed among the planar wallcoverings.

Trade Show Booths

We use the opportunities presented by commercial design trade
shows to merchandize our products in creative and compelling tempo-
rary architecture. In 1997, Ali Tayar with Desai/Chia Architecture designed
a booth that featured rotating panels in a clean composition, inviting
interaction and discovery; for regional trade shows, Eric Mailaender of
Resistance Design created a unique honeycomb steel box that opened
to a clever display and table; our Upholstery booth of 2014 focused on a
single message via a twenty-foot-long sofa flaunting seven richly colored
textiles; and Boym Partners developed an experiential walk-through
"fun house" booth in 2015 to present digital print wallcoverings.

Portable trade show booth, designed by Resistance Design

Booth, designed by Ali Tayar with Desai/Chia Architecture

Fun House booth, designed by Boym Partners

Exquisite Wink

To promote Wink clear dry-erase coating we invoked the Surrealist game of Exquisite Corpse. The booth featured connected drawings, based on the theme of landscape, by seven teams: Michael Graves, Ali Tayar, Snarkitecture, Myles Karr, Ben Katchor, karlssonwilker, and Boym Partners. The unfinished drawings, on vertical panels of painted drywall, wall-covering, aluminum, and wood, were coated in Wink, which allowed visitors to draw over or complete the unfinished works. A condensed version of the booth—the Exquisite Wink board game—shares the artfulness and potential of Wink with design specifiers across the country.

Board game

Fine Art

In 1999, as part of the exhibition *ModernStarts: Places*, the Museum
of Modern Art asked us to re-create a wallpaper pattern from Hector
Guimard's iconic Castel Béranger of 1898. The French architect's
Art Nouveau swirls were engineered into a repeat and produced as
screenprinted wallpaper that was both exhibited and offered for sale
in the museum's Design Store. In 2003, artist Christine Tarkowski
conceived wallcovering as fine art at UCLA's Perloff Gallery and the
Museum of Contemporary Art, Chicago. Three digital printed patterns,
inspired by seventeenth-century French landscape models, spoke to
surveillance in a post-9/11 world.

Main staircase, Castel Béranger, screenprinted wallpaper for MoMA

09:2 installation, designed by Christine Tarkowski, Perloff Gallery, UCLA School of Architecture

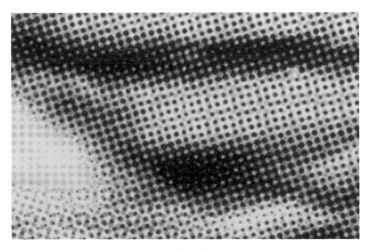

09:2 detail, designed by Christine Tarkowski

The Importance of Erasure

In February 2016, we commissioned British artist Charlotte Mann to draw on a gallery wall in Gowanus, Brooklyn. The project began as a concept, developed by AHOY Studios, for an ad campaign promoting the potential of Wink clear dry-erase coating. Mann's dense layering of patterns found in nature and the built environment—plywood, chain-link fence, willow leaves, and a quilt on a clothesline—demonstrated that, in the creative process, erasure is just as important as leaving a mark.

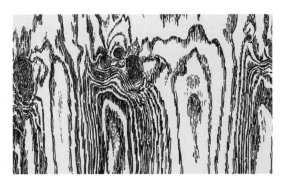

Dining by Design

Tables for DIFFA's annual fundraiser are a prized collaboration between Wolf-Gordon, architect Ali Tayar, and *Interior Design* magazine. Tayar explored perspective in three consecutive installations inspired by the work of Damien Hirst, Leonardo da Vinci, and Jasper Johns. Observed from different angles, these tables, crisply printed through digital means by Wolf-Gordon, teach the secrets of perspective drawing as they draw diners into their trompe l'oeil effects.

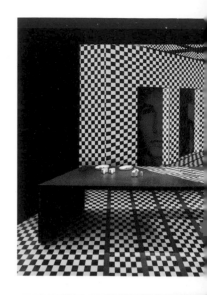

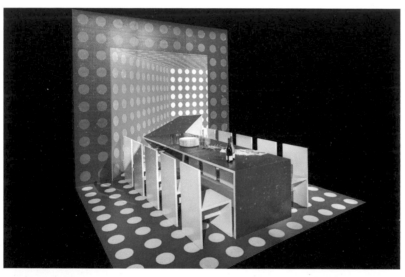

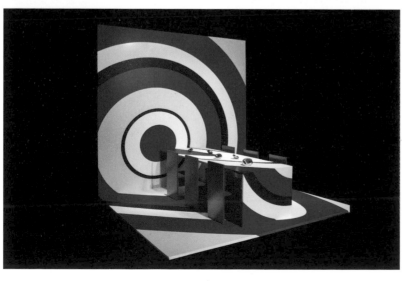

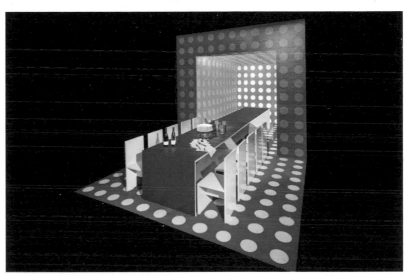

Gift of Hope

Those who worked in interior design in the late 1980s and 1990s could not help but be affected by the many colleagues lost to the AIDS pandemic. In response, Wolf-Gordon created the Gift of Hope program, which directs a percentage of sales proceeds to DIFFA, one of the largest supporters of direct care for people living with HIV/AIDS. In 2013, in recognition of more than two decades of service and more than $1.6 million in contributions, Rick Wolf received a special Unsung Hero Award from the organization.

"I want to make a DIFFArence"

RICK WOLF
President, Wolf-Gordon

Specify With Care®

Specify With Care®, DIFFA's cause marketing program, invites companies to designate a collection or collections and donate a percentage from sales of those to the Foundation. Support from Specify With Care® Affiliates ensures that DIFFA has the resources to help HIV/AIDS organizations year-round and respond quickly to the needs of the organizations it supports.

Rick Wolf, whose company Wolf-Gordon Inc. is a pioneer in the program and DIFFA's single largest contributor, states, "This program is a win-win proposition. It associates manufacturers' names with a good cause and, at the same time, effectively differentiates their products. The interior design and architectural communities are supporting Specify With Care® with overwhelming enthusiasm and optimism."

For more information contact Steven Williams at swilliams@diffa.org. Visit diffa.org for details on all programs.   MEDIA SPONSOR

SURFACE MATTERS

Paul Makovsky

Early in the iconic film *The Graduate,* Dustin Hoffman, as Ben, receives some notable career advice:

Mr. McGuire: I just want to say one word to you. Just one word.

Ben: Yes, sir.

Mr. McGuire: Are you listening?

Ben: Yes, I am.

Mr. McGuire: Plastics.

At the time—1967—even Mr. McGuire couldn't have imagined the sheer range and importance that plastic would come to have. In one summer, over 50 million people visited Expo 67 in Montreal, the highlight of which was Buckminster Fuller's mammoth plastic geodesic dome for the U.S. Pavilion. During the day, its acrylic skin sparkled in the sunlight; at night, the interior gave off a vari-colored glow. The structure encapsulated the country's enthusiasm for technology, progress, and the future. In furniture and interiors, a similar shift was taking place, one that embraced plastic and the artificial. Furniture like the Panton Chair and Blow Chair celebrated the possibilities of plastic as a material for everyday living—the

former in its range of colors, the latter in its promotion of a lightweight, disposable way of living.

The year 1967 was also a good one for Bernie Gordon and Mel Wolf. Wolf and Gordon, along with Tony Prota and Frank Carr, who founded Wolf-Gordon at 132 West Twenty-first Street in New York City, saw that using a vinyl plastic as wallcovering was a new idea, one suited to the times. Architects and interior designers wanted a product that could stand up to abuse by everyone from stockbrokers to hospital professionals. "If you put it on the wall, you wouldn't have to touch it for ten years; whereas with paint, every two or three years you'd have to take a room out of use for upkeep," explains Bernie Gordon. "End users didn't want to be bothered with that." Responding to that need, Wolf-Gordon would design and release a few dozen patterns every year. Durable and high-performing, they also closely reflected the trends and fashions of the times.

The era was one of enormous techno-logical and social upheaval in America. The space race was on, and American culture focused on Vietnam, the Cold War, NASA, and speedy jet airplanes. American stores like Design Research introduced colorful geometric textiles from the Finnish company Marimekko; flower power was in full force in the hand-dyed paisley and floral fabrics young globetrotters brought home from India and other far-flung locales. Rachel Carson's famous call-to-arms *Silent Spring* was published in 1962, awakening Americans to environmental issues.

Wolf-Gordon's lines of the late 1960s embodied all of these attributes and more. The Vinyls Inc Series C catalog presented wallcoverings, wall fabrics, and upholstery textiles that mimicked materials found in nature: cork (Granada Cork, Madrid Cork, and Corticiera), stone (Calcutta and Calais), and even Rodin Marble. Natural woven grass fabrics—Yangtze Grass, Karoonda Grass, Jakata Straw, Burlap, Nepal Burlap, and Luchow Silk—were popular staples for the company. Other nature-inspired materials included collections based on Pacific Northwest flora (Oregon Grass and Yakima Grass) and North American tree bark (Indian Trail, Prairie Grass, and Seneca Silk).

Swinging London was also a major influence on fashion, music, style, and design in the 1960s, especially with famous exports like the Rolling Stones, Pink Floyd, and the Who. A wave of eccentric, contemporary trends from Carnaby and Kensington Streets offered a youthful, modern style. Wolf-Gordon's textile wallcoverings recalled the elegance of London's classic looks and the impeccable tailoring of Savile Row. Tweed and wool lines took names from the British Isles (Limerick, Norwich, and Dundee). Eton, a good, traditional pattern, was branded as a "vin-a-lar stain resistant wallcovering coated with Du Pont Tedlar"—it could be wiped clean like ceramic tile. Velvetlike Crush and Gotham Suede (in brown "cloven hoof") and Union Stripe, an almost invisible striation, were other refined suit fabric looks available in somber colors.

Wolf-Gordon also named several patterns after booming American cities. The colorways of Dallas (Canoli, Scampi, Cappuccino, Marsala, Burgundy Red, Prawn, Bing Cherry, Mushroom, Souffle, Chianti, Madeira, Romano, Chestnut, and Artichoke) read like a menu

from the city's high-end restaurant Town & Country, which prided itself on "cuisine française" for discriminating diners. (The dining room featured a special stand for its nine-foot pepper mill.) Orlando shared the cool, modernist palette—bone, off white, and shades of blue—of a 1960s prefab bungalow. And Palm Beach Patent, available in especially descriptive shades (Doublemint, Siamese Pink, and Gold Digger, my favorite), would have blended perfectly into an interior like the Corvette Room, the luxuriously informal circular dining room at La Coquille Club at the Ritz-Carlton Hotel in Palm Beach.

The arts of the time, notably the Pop Art movement that celebrated imagery from mass media and popular culture as well as commonplace objects, also infiltrated Wolf-Gordon's designs. The concept that art could borrow from any source was one of the most influential characteristics of Pop Art, and in the case of Wolf-Gordon, the company's designs would arise from a wide range of origins. High Society Patent, an expanded elastic-backed wallcovering, for example, embodied the glossy coated leather that was popular for 1960s handbags, kinky boots, shoes, and trench coats. It came in strong, bold colors, ranging from shades of black (Pine Tree, Cochese, and Smoke), blue (Aqua Spray, Spectre Blue, Dresden Blue, and Sea Turquoise), and green (Kelly Green, Johnson Green, Avocado, and Lime) to yellow (Slicker Yellow, Buttercup, and Gold) and pink (Pink Elephant, Cameo Pink, Apricot Flip, and Baby Pink). The rosy hues, in particular, reflected a fascination with India explicated by *Vogue* editor Diana Vreeland: "Pink is the navy blue of India."

Yet another current of the 1960s was a rebellious countercultural attitude. In contrast to the pure, modernist "Good Design" of the previous decade, new social norms valued individuality—once the prerogative of the wealthy, the famous, and the beautiful—over conformity. During the Summer of Love, as many as a hundred thousand hippies converged on the Haight-Ashbury neighborhood of San Francisco. Flower children inhabiting communes favored bright colors and dynamic graphic patterns. Lines like Calcutta drew a connection to polyphonic Hindu and Buddhist spirituality.

Hues of aubergine, violet, and fuchsia, sunshine yellow, indigo blue, and orange set off the explosion of color that would come to characterize interiors by the turn of the 1970s. Large-scale geometric forms, or Supergraphics, often splashed on surfaces in diagonals or curving shapes in bright primary colors, electrified walls and floors. At the same time, earth tones ruled. Hippie culture had evolved from its garish beginnings to a back-to-the-land vibe, and the first Earth Day took place in 1970. Author Tom Wolfe identified yet another quality of the era—the transition from basic materialism to conspicuous consumption—when he dubbed the 1970s the "Me Decade." Across the board, new ways of thinking—feminism, gay liberation, environmentalism—shifted society's preconceptions.

Wolf-Gordon's Valencia catalog of 1975 demonstrated a newly developed concept in textured natural cork wallcovering: the cork veneer was carefully laminated onto a cloth backing. Patterns evoking natural-looking grasses, already popular, evolved into more intricate arrangements: Acapulco resembled mixed grasses in contrasting colors; Myrtle Beach and Hemp evoked a handcrafted feeling in rough, exaggerated patterns; and Haverstraw had a tighter patterned weave. The crafted and irregularly woven Yangtze and Mondo Grass patterns recalled Asian folk art techniques, while Savannah, Hawaiian Grass, and South Seas pointed to lightweight wallcoverings that worked well in almost any setting.

Colors like avocado (the most popular color of 1972), harvest gold, and burnt orange strongly influenced color trends. Fashions ranged from suede-on-suede to disco queen lamé and towering platforms. Faux wood grains, alluding to the one-story ranch house, became sought-after designs for wallcoverings, and Wolf-Gordon offered a wide range of options: North American and exotic classic woods, black walnut, Thai teak, rosewood, and Spanish oak, to name just a few. The company also presented more specialized treated woods like limed pecan, aged pecan, and Argentine oak. Others had a western feeling: Ponderosa, Some House, Barnboard, Buckeye, and Conestoga all recalled the rough-hewn planks that adorned the sets of *Bonanza* and *Little House on the Prairie*.

The classic tailoring of the 1960s, an important influence, had become more sophisticated a decade later. Patterned textures included the browns and grays of Valiant Stripe, Malibu Suede, and the corduroy-like Korda Suede. Concorde Chevron Suede depicted a minimalist pyramidal pattern with strict geometric lines that gave it both texture and pattern.

Some of Wolf-Gordon's designs evoked escapist fantasies. One faux-suede-based series related to swashbuckling adventurers: Buccaneer (which became one of the company's best sellers), Musketeer, Cavalier, Castaway, and Shipwreck (pirates, anyone?) ranged in color from rich reds (Persimmon, Scarlett, Amber, Cinnamon, Flamingo, and Brick) to earthy browns (Teak, Saddle, Spice, Tabac, Sable, Cocoa, Cordovan, and Sienna).

Wolf-Gordon's wild side manifested in its Wild Kingdom collection. The replicated animal hides included those of crocodiles and alligators, tortoises and snakes. Thankfully no animals were harmed in the making of these vinyl upholstery fabrics. By the mid-1970s, the Wolf-Gordon Vinyls Collection had expanded to include dozens of lines in thousands of patterns and colors.

The belief in a technologically driven future saw the rise of consumer products, often miniaturized, like Cuisinarts, eight-track tapes, Betamax videotapes, and pocket calculators. These labor-saving devices allowed more time for video games, like Pong, or disco dancing to the Bee Gees or Donna Summer. The disco, with its flashing strobe lights, high-energy music, and mirror balls, symbolized an excessive and hedonistic lifestyle, and in 1976, there were tens of thousands of them in the United States. Wolf-Gordon provided reflective surfaces appropriate for any fantastical setting: Mercury Mylar was patterned in silver, gold, copper, and brushed silk; Jupiter echoed an otherworldliness in a deliberately artificial-looking stone surface; and Lunar, another stony-looking landscape surface, gave prominence to a range of hues from off-white, eggshell, and mist to blues and avocado green.

By the 1980s, the bright, over-lit interiors of the 1970s had given way to softer, more muted rooms. Architects began to use more color, and to use it differently, in buildings and interiors. The *AIA Journal* wrote, in 1978, that younger architects "have been looking more seriously at a wider range of color choices. Not only the bright pigments of high-tech and supergraphics. Not only the eggshell pastels of Beaux-Arts. And not only the woodsy rich tones of High Victorian. But even the sweet seagreens of the '50s," according to Sara O. Marberry, author of *Color in the Office*.

The 1980s saw globalization and advances in technology contribute to great societal shifts. The early part of the decade was marked by a severe global recession; just a few years later, the stock market and laissez-faire government policies fostered an economic and housing surge across the country. A "greed is good" attitude saw an increase in corporate takeovers, leveraged buyouts, and mergers and acquisitions. Maturing baby boomers—the "Masters of the Universe" in another of Wolfe's turns of phrase—discovered nesting. The crafty spirit of the 1970s shifted to a more voyeuristic, unbridled consumerist attitude. Nancy Reagan told America's youth to "Just Say No"; America's youth replied, "I want my MTV." The range of design styles was similarly unfettered: preppy influences with classic blue and white stripes; palettes of soft pastels; the return of florals and cabbage rose chintzes; the rise of slick, edgy minimalism; and the architectural influences of Memphis and postmodernism.

One of Wolf-Gordon's most important collections was Metropole: fifteen screen-printed patterns in seventy-five colorways on three standard backgrounds. Developed by Patty Madden in 1982, this collection was Wolf-Gordon's most complex to date. Rick Wolf explains that interior designers could use screen printing to customize vinyl wallcovering. "It was nice to come out with something unique, to bring real design and color to vinyl," Madden says. The collection was manufactured to create a handcrafted look, and the company announced that its experienced screen printers would be able to customize designs such as company logos or trademarks. The Squadrons pattern

looked like planes in flight formations and could be printed on Suffolk Suede, Nassau Stucco, or Westchester Suede. Other patterns reflected important cultural signifiers of the early 1980s: Wall Street featured random ticks in a wavelike formation; the flying elements of Missile Command were perhaps a nod to Ronald Reagan's "mutually assured destruction." Sputnik and Galaxy were pre-occupied with space, while Pick-Up-Sticks playfully and primitively replicated computer technology.

The rise of personal computing in this period would transform society. IBM unveiled its first PC in 1981, and Apple introduced the Macintosh in 1984. (It wasn't until 1990, though, that the term *wallpaper* migrated from walls to computers.) Fax machines, voice mail, and cell phones transformed communications, promising a world that was faster, easier, more convenient. Wolf-Gordon's Summit collection incorporated tech-driven trends: GRID moved beyond straight lines; Edgemont and Kernel exhibited indented and rounded squares, respectively; and Vanguard was formed of a relief of floating squares. Hi Tek Tile reproduced tiny, almost pixel-like patterns on a solid background. The New Wave collection preserved the high-tech minimalist look but in contemporary colors— metallics, stones, and faux fabrics—that were applicable in almost any setting, bold or classic, commercial or residential.

The Fantastex collection of "hi-tec" expanded vinyl wallcovering presented minimalist tactile surface effects via textured geometric gridded patterns in whites, grays, and beiges. Promotional photos paired the patterns with classic early modernist furniture, such as Rietveld's Red and Blue chair. Pattern 9092 was a case in point: a module of four squares with one a solid square; the design, when used on a larger scale, almost produced an early computer special effect.

Popular television sagas like *Dallas, Dynasty,* and *Knots Landing* showcased wealthy families in which the women espoused shoulder pads, wide lapels, and hairstyles that evinced an attitude of "the higher the hair, the closer to God." Wolf-Gordon's mylar mirrored surfaces of the 1970s evolved into more luxuriously reflective and intricately composed surfaces by means of high-tech, machine-made, decorative stamping. Among the sumptuous metallic patterns were Midas Mylar, a range of silvers and golds—described as Flute, Puff Diamond, Holiday, Deep Crush, Gangee, and Block—as well as brushed platinum, copper, pewter, and a metallic brushed silk. Xanadu—likely based on the 1980 film promoted as "A Fantasy, A Musical, A Place Where Dreams Come True"—was another fantastical pattern available in pinks (Mauve Dust, Pale Rose, and Brick Rose), neutral grays, and blues (Powder, Ore, Blueberry, and Blue Mountain). The faux animal and reptile patterns of the 1970s were magnified and augmented in the 1980s. No longer intended as true depictions of land or sea creatures, the skins were accentuated with various colors: pale neutrals, whites of different hues, pearlized salmon, lilac, "Zane Grey," metallic silver, gunmetal, and black.

Another influence in the period was postmodern architectural theory, which fueled a desire for ornament, a return to the past, eclecticism, and an attitude of "more is more." Michael Graves, Robert Venturi, and Philip Johnson—all proponents of the style—employed large-scale ornamentation to celebrate luxurious materials and abstract forms in the creation of a new language that married modernism and classicism. The color palette shifted to one character-ized by an association with nature: terra cotta symbolized the earth; gray represented stone; greens, the landscape; and blues, the sky. Decorative columns, pilasters, pediments, bases, and moldings—whether true replicas or simply representational forms—became an important source for both pattern and architecture. The Ritz collection combined elegance and beauty, artistry and grace, with distinctive prints and borders. Regency Border portrayed the new historicism at its most deluxe: it would be at home in any Wall Street office, brokerage firm, or power restaurant. Victoria, part of the Kings Pointe collection, depicted a historical dimensional foliage damask pattern with Victorian leaf scrolls on an antique crackled background. The handcrafted approach was evident in the Olympus collection, described as "very fine Italian textile wallcoverings with a unique decorating concept that combined the characteristic warm and depths effects of woven textiles and yarns with the most up to date artisanal production." This artisanal approach was evident in the Pinebrook series as well—"Traditional meets Off-beat," as Wolf-Gordon described it—an eclectic mix of prints, textures, and stripes mirroring trends in 1980s interior design. Seafan—a series of stacked fans in a pastel rainbow of pale green, rose, and blue gray—would look equally good on the set of *Miami Vice* or *The Golden Girls*. The Premier Collection of Natural Fibres—woven linens, grasses, reeds, cottons, silks, and exotic wallcoverings—was hand-made by skilled artisans, which meant that the tension of the warp was not consistent, since no two craftsmen produce a uniform fabric. The unique character of the finished product was a strong selling point for Wolf-Gordon. The company pointed out that the delicate shadings varied from roll to roll and even within the roll, ensuring that each pattern would appear distinctive. Linen reflected the crisp, high-fashion fabrics of the time; Chevron consisted of alternating stripes of white and brown and cotton-nubby woven patterns that ranged from rough to smooth; and Grass Cloth was distinguished by single strands of grass held in place by thin cotton thread in natural beige and browns.

The influence of the Memphis Group— founded by Italian Ettore Sottsass and including an international roster of designers—inspired bizarre, bright looks and bold geometric patterns. The designers and their products influenced not only mass culture but fashionable brands like Fiorucci and Esprit and even the graphics for MTV. Normandy was one of the Wolf-Gordon collections that showed Memphis-inspired design. The border pattern Alpine consisted of an abstract mountain broken into basic geometric elements in pastel colors. Luxor Vinyl—patterns included Sahara, Dune, Oases, Egypt, Pyramids, and Nile Delta—was another collection with a Memphis-like attitude toward mixing stone textures and light palettes.

Soft pastels reigned supreme in the 1980s, and if two colors were emblematic of the decade, they would have to be mauve and gray. As the 1990s approached, however, muted pastels—teals, taupes, and purples like eggplant and the fancier "aubergine"—gained prominence. Brown was back, and black, in a backlash against bright pomo colors, became a signifier of status, luxury, and power. Richly saturated jewel tones, like those in the Melrose collection, also became popular choices.

Another trend of the times was soothing and spiritual Japanese-inspired patterns. Osaka and Osaka Border—part of the Sutton Place collection—included a dado rail with decorative fans. The playful composition could be mixed and matched with other Sutton Place patterns like Tokyo (snowflakes in a blizzard) and Geisha (floating fans with ribbons).

The 1990s, in contrast to the go-go freneticism of the previous decade, were all about retreating: scaling back, toning down, and returning to basics. The economy slumped into recession, and gone were the excess and glitz of the 1980s, gone were the frills, the froufrou canopy beds, and the linebacker-scaled shoulder pads. A new minimalism in interiors was serene, minimal, and soothing, often with sensuous textures. When it came to contract settings, David Gordon explains, "Back in the early nineties, the philosophy of the interior designers was to keep the wall decoration simple. They would choose the carpet and furniture first and then let the walls complement and not clash with all their furnishings." Solid patterns and those imitating faux stones and looks from nature were popular successes. Attention to issues like sustainability and the influence of the green movement—"reduce, reuse, recycle"—positioned the company strongly in the market. Faux finishes offered a logical alternative to luxurious and expensive natural stones and marbles, and the company's imitations could fool even the most trained eye.

Wolf-Gordon's birth and adolescence, like so many companies in the contract interiors industry, followed fashions of the day. The majority of patterns from the early decades were based on nature, designed to look like something else—stone, wood, grasses, animal skins—and seen as affordable substitutes for more costly materials. A turning point for the company came in 1995, when the second generation of family management took over. Rick Wolf, David Gordon, and Rob Wolf embarked on a series of initiatives focused on building up the Wolf-Gordon sales force and creating exclusive designs. National sales managers Mike Gorelick and Mark Mendlen and vice president of design and marketing Marybeth Shaw joined the company in 1997. The renewed entrepreneurial spirit and determination to grow the enterprise—accompanied by fresh strategies for designing, communicating, and selling—would help transform Wolf-Gordon from, as Rick Wolf says, a company that sold design into a design company.

MAKING IT REAL

Melissa Feldman

The Art of Thought, a groundbreaking volume outlining the four stages of the creative process, was radical for its time. Written in 1926 by Graham Wallas, a British scholar and social psychologist, the book sets out the stages of *preparation,* the initial gathering of thoughts; *incubation,* when a detachment with the process takes hold; *illumination,* the aha moment; and finally, *verification,* when an idea gels.

Applied to contemporary practice, Wallas's almost-century-old framework seems obvious. Yet at Wolf-Gordon, where the creative process often involves visionaries, a somewhat different approach often takes hold. Since the late 1990s, the wallcovering and upholstery company has conjured up a series of initiatives that extend well beyond the products that are manufactured and sold to revolve around marketing, publicity, and philanthropy. The innovative intellects who are commissioned by the brand traverse the stages of the creative process in conjunction with the brand, witnessing their designs condensed and purified, challenged by various knotty,

technical issues, before emerging as a collective idea. The process, coaxed and prodded by Marybeth Shaw, vice president of design and marketing, builds until consensus is achieved. Sometimes a few curve balls—a budget limitation or particular request—are thrown into the mix, yet the continuum moves inexorably forward.

Wolf-Gordon's visual campaigns are centered on annual themes established by Shaw and an experienced yet nuanced team of global talent. Communications tools, such as sales booklets, online strategies, and even holiday ornaments, are tended to by a select group of multidisciplinary design studios: Stefan Sagmeister, 2x4, Anthony Russell, AHOY Studios, and most recently, karlssonwilker. Additionally, a network of architects, fabricators, and printers are regularly called upon to manufacture larger assemblies including showrooms, trade show booths, and national and international installations.

According to Hjalti Karlsson, one of two partners in karlssonwilker, a project begins with a phone call, then discussion, then a detailed design brief from Shaw. Some undertakings are fairly wide open; others are more defined. Stationery, business cards, sample books, tip cards, and folders typically follow predetermined sizes and formats. But for the redesign of the website in 2015, there was a sense of diving into the unknown. Karlsson describes the first meeting, in which the discussion revolved around the necessity of creating a sense of place, or spatial quality, for the site. "The process was open, and we came back with a couple of ideas," says Karlsson. The team finally settled on a tabletop-like array of product samples to convey a sense of space and dimensionality. "It's always like this," he says about the growth and nurturing of ideas. "Someone will have a spark, then it goes from there."

Karlsson and his partner, Jan Wilker, maintain that the overall approach is occasionally linear, often organic, and sometimes entirely indeterminate. Digital technology has become a vital tool, and the workflow varies from month to month. "It doesn't feel old," says Karlsson about his relationship with Wolf-Gordon. "It's unpredictable, but there's trust and respect from both sides."

One of the biggest open-ended design efforts each year is NeoCon, the annual trade show at Chicago's Merchandise Mart. Built by Marshall Field & Co. in the late 1920s, the Mart has four million square feet devoted to approximately 1,200 permanent showrooms, including Wolf-Gordon's. Designers visit year-round to scope out the latest home and office furnishings. But NeoCon is the fount of all contract fairs where manufacturers, designers, architects—anyone in commercial interior design—endure a few muggy days in Chicago during the second week of June. And every year Wolf-Gordon launches an interactive experience.

Starting in 2012, Wolf-Gordon has installed a hanging sculpture—unique for each year—that becomes the foundation for the annual cycle of the company's advertising and marketing materials. For the first iteration, Shaw was inspired by the faceted dome of Bruno Taut's Glass Pavilion of 1914; she also wanted upholstery textiles to be displayed as prominently as wallcoverings. Samples of fabrics and wallcoverings were applied to the faces of the crystalline form. For the 2015 sculpture, SLICE, digital screens suspended above the Mart escalator recorded and transmuted the motions of fairgoers, capturing data that was used to produce a digital wallcovering later that year.

Wolf-Gordon's trade advertising campaign is generated by the NeoCon installation. A series of full-page ads traces the evolution of the sculpture from loose concept to determined theme to final realization. Karlsson says, "The first ad in January is really just a sketch based on early discussions, though the sketch in fact drives the design of the sculpture for the coming June." That first ad is often an abstract image, one that a consumer perusing a magazine might not immediately comprehend. By the time the June promotion appears, the sculpture has crystallized; in the second half of the year, the ads zoom to photographic details of specific products.

Beyond NeoCon, the contract interiors industry is characterized by a series of trade shows in the United States and overseas. In 2000, Eric Mailaender of Resistance Design was hired to create a portable trade show stand for smaller, regional shows. "The brief was interesting in that the mission was to circumvent hiring local workers to assemble the show space. Something light and compact that could be carried in and assembled without tools," says Mailaender. He developed two boxes manufactured from aluminum honeycomb panels and stainless steel. The stand is carried in on shoulder straps and assembled by hand. Mailaender's design also incorporates a kinetic feature: fabric samples are mounted on blocks with rods, encouraging visitors to touch and rotate them.

Wolf-Gordon's permanent showrooms are devised by means of a similar thoughtful process. In order to translate the company's products into practical terms, in 1999 Shaw enlisted Baratloo-Balch Architects to design a showroom in Manhattan's D&D Building, one of the city's centers for design showrooms. The Mondrian-inspired display includes over 560 framed samples hung in the spirit of an eighteenth-century salon. According to Balch, the samples provide a visual index to the entire Wolf-Gordon collection, with identification labels cross-referencing product numbers in catalogs. The modular frames, in four sizes to accommodate patterns at different scales, have been updated to incorporate three-dimensional forms for upholstery presentation. More than a decade after its inception, the space still looks and functions as if it were brand new. "It's a testament to the architects' core design that the showroom still looks fresh and accommodates the newer product lines," says Shaw.

Istanbul-born architect Ali Tayar worked on multiple interventions for Wolf-Gordon, including an exhibition booth and tableaus for charitable causes such as DIFFA (Design Industries Foundation Fighting AIDS). Tayar's inspiration for tablescapes for the annual Dining by Design fundraiser originated from art history coupled with Expressionist architecture, which he was introduced to at the University of Stuttgart and at MIT. Shaw, who also has a degree from the rigorous Boston-area institution, and Tayar have created a laboratory model with concepts and innovations that the company now explores.

Tayar's patterned environments, produced for Dining by Design cosponsors Wolf-Gordon and *Interior Design* magazine, utilize digital printed wallcovering. Among the artistic themes explored by the architect are Jasper Johns's targets, Leonardo da Vinci's *Last Supper,* and Damien Hirst's "pharmaceutical" spot paintings. The wallcovering extends over a table and chairs for a dozen guests and even onto the floor. "It's a lot of material and man hours," says Tayar.

In reference to the various approaches to Wolf-Gordon's equally various production, Shaw says, "As a company that designs across several product categories for the creatively receptive design community, we have latitude to explore different 2-D, 3-D, and virtual devices. Yet it is also important to tie projects together thematically and across media." One visual device—the Ad Sculptures, for instance—ties into the design and promotion of new wallcoverings while also opening new directions for future company-wide strategies. Repurposing samples from each season's product patterns and morphing them into a series of design

interventions—promotions, branding, and specialty products as well as philanthropic efforts—has become part of the company's master plan.

It is perhaps the incubation stage as established in Wallas's *Art of Thought* that is most meaningful for Shaw and her creative collaborators. Working within a group dynamic allows each participant time to contemplate the outcome, while brainstorming generates new ideas and initiatives throughout the year and for coming years. "The repetition of a sound conceptual framework allows for ultimate variation in content as products evolve," says Shaw. "As part of that evolution, our clients become more confident in our ability to provide them with products beyond wallcoverings and at the same time more charmed by the methods we use to communicate design."

FLOWERS OF THE WALL

Ellen Lupton

In 2003, a *Fortune* magazine feature heralded the rebirth of "style-impaired" products like washing machines and padlocks as sexy objects of desire. On the opening spread, Karim Rashid gazes out from a full-bleed photograph. Dressed in his signature white suit, the Egyptian-born designer lounges on a succulent pink chair, his legs akilter in a confident manspread. Commanding the foreground are Rashid's enormous feet, clad in bulky white leather shoes with techy straps (NASA meets Birkenstock). Dominating the background is an undulating pattern from Rashid's 2002 Digital Nature collection, designed for Wolf-Gordon.

The phrase "dominating the background" may be an oxymoron. Background and foreground compete against each other in a temporal battlefield of perception. At any given moment, our attention focuses on one element at the expense of the others. Center and periphery constantly switch places as our restless eyes shuttle from one narrow point of interest to the next. The mind builds a dynamic representation of reality from these thousands of tiny targets. The background,

by definition, must blur and recede, taking its place behind and between the objects of our gaze. We live, these days, in an attention economy that races to "capture eyeballs" and convince consumers to see, like, and follow countless minute particles set loose in a foaming stratosphere of content and keywords. To design a wallcovering is to push past attention and design a background—a surface that willingly withdraws. A thoughtfully designed pattern dissolves the walls around us into a loosely knit enclosure, a rough-edged clearing.

Yet in order to penetrate the consciousness of the architects and interior designers who decide how to cover our walls, a pattern cannot merely recede. It must come forward and tell a story. Since 2001, Wolf-Gordon has licensed designers from outside the specialty of surface design to create patterns that disrupt our expectations about how wallcoverings ought to look and behave. Collections designed by Rashid, Laurinda Spear, Petra Blaisse, Boym Partners, Morgan Bajardi, Frank Tjepkema, Grethe Sørensen, and others demand attention and sing their own songs. They stimulate the eye and intrigue the imagination. Even so, each Wolf-Gordon collection performs across multiple registers. Rashid's writhing magenta Replicant became a darling of the press, while his Flexuous pattern printed in pale pearl or sterling eases the mind and body into a gentler state of habitation.

Marybeth Shaw, vice president of design and marketing at Wolf-Gordon, guides designers through the unique challenges of inventing backgrounds, helping them create pattern families that include quiet flowers of the wall as well as attention-seeking stars. When she joined Wolf-Gordon in 1997, Shaw recognized that contract wallcoverings were stuck in a rut—bland, formulaic, obsessed with faux effects and timid washes of color. Commissioning designers to create new, experimental designs was a way to shake up this sleepy product space. She explains, "Our partner designers regularly infuse our collections with fresh ideas on design, scale, and color. They challenge us to keep a part of our product line experimental and engaged in the continuum of design. Wolf-Gordon needs to *participate* in design, bringing our interior design customers new concepts that they have not yet thought of or seen." The back-and-forth design process is targeted toward creating functional and inspiring collections that push Wolf-Gordon in new directions. These curated collections are not expected to be the company's top sellers; instead, they inform its standard product line and reinforce Wolf-Gordon's role as a leader in American design.

Shaw launched her first licensed collection, Linework, with the Miami-based architect Laurinda Spear in 2001. Cofounder of the firm Arquitectonica, Spear designs landscapes, furniture, and fabrics as well as buildings. Already familiar with the demands of conceiving interior surfaces, Spear spun out a series of strong yet workable patterns. The diagonal ribs of Palmrail suggest palm fronds converging into wide, curved stripes that snake relentlessly upward. Wave, from the same collection, has interlocking nodes that bulge out like the toe pads of a tree frog, while Bamboo builds graphic planks out of stacks of oblique lines. Spear's second collection, Geo Graphic, was inspired by natural materials and built environments. Endgrain recalls the cut ends of raw lumber, while Urban Steel resembles Giambattista Nolli's famous eighteenth-century maps of positive and negative urban space. These motifs proved that graphic patterns and strong colors could disrupt the dull beige world of contract wallcoverings.

While Rashid expanded Spear's graphic precedent with lavish, computer-generated wireframes, Dutch designer Petra Blaisse introduced an entirely new vocabulary with her Touch collection of 2003. Hyperdetailed photographs of wool, felt, fur, and stitched and knitted fabrics—which maximize detail and dimensionality—create "honestly fake" surfaces. Exactingly printed in rotogravure, each texture appears warm, fuzzy, and soft to the touch. Blaisse's architectural curtains—many commissioned by Rem Koolhaas—exploit pattern, texture, and inventive hardware. These fabric walls move, breathe, and change. "What fascinates me most in design is the potential of boundaries," explains Blaisse. "This wallcovering collection illustrates the interactive play between design and the spectator, giving the latter the idea of the wall being a soft and three-dimensional material, challenging him to come closer and touch it." Indeed, when confronted with a Touch wall in person, viewers can't help but come close and test its stunning illusion. Shaw explains, "Petra created soft, ambiguous borders for rooms that played with one's perception of the limits of interior spaces." Diverse colorways transform the patterns' meaning and impact. Neutral and bleached shades emphasize the textures' natural origins, while bright colors like pink (grapeseed) and blue (ocean) celebrate an aesthetic of simulation. The black and white variants of Touch transport us into a different world altogether, one of representation rather than simulation—ink on paper, motion pictures, silver gelatin photography.

Constantin and Laurene Boym took a more narrative journey with their Recollections series, launched in 2015. The Boyms' work is rich with humor and cultural references. Their Buildings of Disaster series offers collectors tiny souvenir replicas of architectural monuments associated with terror and wrongdoing, from the failed Three Mile Island nuclear reactors to the World Trade Center and the Unabomber's cabin. (The latter is also the subject of a wooden birdhouse, which is in the collection of John Waters.) The Boyms design utilitarian items as well as symbolic objects, including flatware for Gourmet Settings based on army surplus, gothic films, and the mismatched contents of a family silverware drawer. Memory—personal and shared—plays a role in all the Boyms' work, and indeed each pattern in Recollections is a visual souvenir of places the designers have visited. The dotted-line arabesques in Jaipur contain hidden references to Indian animals and deities; the bright staccato rectangles of Venice recall the glass mosaics of that port city; and Broadway offers a gleeful and glamorous interpretation of New York's most beloved tourist industry. The graphics of Jaipur and Venice are flat, but Broadway pulls us in deep, its illusionistic folds becoming a stage set for the viewer's personal drama. Constantin Boym explains, "Decoration still has a somewhat tainted reputation since modernism tried to discredit it in the twentieth century. Glimpses of the real world, used as inspiration for patterns, make decoration more interesting, even narrative. You can look at these patterns and imagine a story—or have a recollection!"

Broadway, says Shaw, is ideally suited to corridors and other large expanses of wall. Looping and bending to describe tall columns, the folds become richly three-dimensional stripes. Many patterns across Wolf-Gordon's licensed collections return to the archetypal stripe, from Spear's geometric palm fronds to Rashid's erratic Replicant or Blaisse's soft, fibrous cords. These stripes shimmer, blur, bend, and wander, yet they maintain their sense of rhythmic verticality. Warped grids also prevail. Networks of lines transform from positive to negative, cubic to floral, in Frank Tjepkema's Osmosis and Metamorphosis. His collection, Tjep. Cubism, encompasses woven upholstery and sheer drapery as well as vinyl and textile wallcoverings. Textile designer Morgan Bajardi uses linear wireframes to bend our perception of space. Bajardi's patterns Tall and Wide, based on fashion textiles she created to reshape the female silhouette,

appear to swell upward or outward; this expert textile designer has become an integral member of the Wolf-Gordon Design Studio. Another decorative archetype is the blossom, reexamined as a geometric figure in Tsao & McKown's Flower, from the Passage collection. Like graphic origami, these unfolding buds confront a traditional, naturalistic motif with crisp geometry.

Grethe Sørensen's astonishing group of upholstery fabrics and wallcoverings revisits some of these archetypes. The small sharp pixels in Codes cluster into vertical bands, while the gradient tones in Blinds fade to white with exquisite slowness. The big grid of polka dots in Soft Spots counteracts Pop Art scale with edgeless figures that emerge slowly from an optical fog. The gradient is so subtle that the dots virtually disappear as viewers come in close. Sørensen's atmospheric patterns dissolve the borders of a room. A Danish textile designer who integrates printing and weaving techniques with photography, Sørensen pioneered a method of converting digital pixels into threads for weaving, a technique she has used to stunning effect in her Wolf-Gordon textile Millions of Colors. Designed with an enormous repeat (223.5 inches), the woven wool and nylon fabrics shimmer with gently shifting colors mixed from colored threads. The large repeat makes every upholstered piece a unique object.

Printed wallcoverings traffic in the space between material and immaterial. Each one adds image to architecture, defying the solidity of form and structure with an illusory skin of representation. Patterned surfaces degrade the purity of abstraction with the seductiveness of graphic form. And yet these patterns are more than graphic. They bring tactility to the experience of space; they implicate not just the eye but also the body. Patterned walls construct an envelope of experience where color and texture imply depth, permeability, and change—a place of dwelling.

DESIGNS THAT SELL

Our sales force is highly regarded among interior design specifiers for its experienced, consultative approach. The team is supported in its endeavors by strategies and materials that the discriminating audience finds persuasive and inspiring. Going beyond standard catalog-based product presentation has been an unwavering principle of vice president of sales Mike Gorelick, who happens to be a professional magician on the side. When Gorelick began working for Wolf-Gordon in 1997, he instilled in his sales representatives the importance of meticulous presentation methods and of romancing the product. Fortunately, our marketing department enjoys the challenge of devising innovative ways to introduce new products. Sales tools that delight, coupled with product design that has never stopped improving, result in presentations and products that designers look forward to and remember.

For Wallcovering

One of the first of our unique sales tools was a beautifully crafted steel box with laser-cut "windows." Samples of textile wallcoverings peek out from the apertures. A corresponding giveaway to attendees of Interplan 1997—a mini stack deck on a chain with a laser-cut steel cover— swirled to show thirty different wallcovering samples and doubled as a wearable pendant.

123

For Upholstery

Upholstery collections, added to our line in late 2011, have inspired their own series of sales tools, all of which make the most of fabric's visual and tactile qualities. Russian Dolls presents textile patterns of diverse scales as a series of nested "envelopes" of progressively smaller sizes. A business card, complete with Russian doll graphic, hides in the smallest. Coated upholstery textiles are assembled in the touchable stuffed Parka, which unzips to a linear formation. The Scarf, also known as the Snake, compiles nearly one hundred perfectly sewn upholstery samples in a twelve-foot-long color spectrum.

Perks

Premiums for our customers are characterized by a sense of delight and discovery—a sense that epitomizes our product introductions as well. The It's a Top/It's a Bag convertible tote was printed in the Bankside pattern from London Chic and was, to no one's surprise, an extremely popular gift at the Hospitality Design Expo in Las Vegas. For the same show, graphic designers karlssonwilker designed a deck of playing cards in well-known Wolf-Gordon patterns. Perhaps the giveaways our customers recall most fondly are the plush wolf toys offered between 1998 and 2005.

Infinity

Adire

Textile Wallcovering
56.5" Wide

High performance textile wallcovering made with recycled polyester.

This textile was inspired by a beaded panel from the N'debele people of South Africa, ca 20th century, from the Girard Foundation collection, Museum of International Folk Art, Department of Cultural Affairs, New Mexico. ©Museum of New Mexico.

ADR 9000 Noir

Wolf Gordon

Design inspired by a Museum of New Mexico artifact

Organics

Multi-Materials Wallcovering
36" Wide

Organic Wallcovering made
from PLA, Kenaf and Recycled
Newspapers & Magazines

TAJ 7101   Silver

Wolf Gordon

Organics

Battista

Multi-Materials Wallcovering
36" Wide

Organic Wallcovering made
from PLA, Kenaf and Recycled
Newspapers & Magazines

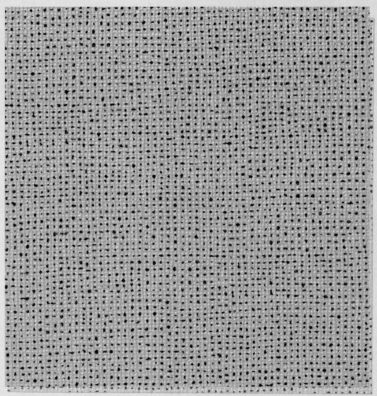

BTT 7201   Kona

Wolf Gordon

Essentials

Stingray
Multi-Materials Wallcovering
54" Width

STY 7-7053   Chamois

Wolf Gordon

Essentials

Twigs

Multi-Materials Wallcovering
54" Width

Designed by
Patty Madden

TWG 7-6900   Bark

© Patty Madden Inc.

Wolf Gordon

Designed by Patty Madden

Haven III

Contemplation

WALLCOVERING | Vinyl | *Designed by Patty Madden*

CTM 9-2159   View

© Patty Madden Inc.

Wolf Gordon

Designed by Patty Madden

Summit
Textures

Network
Vinyl Wallcovering
54" Wide

Designed by
Patty Madden

NWK 7-5468   Plait

Wolf Gordon

Designed by Patty Madden

Haven III

Briarwood

WALLCOVERING | Vinyl | *Designed by Patty Madden*

BRW 9-2218   Tract

© Patty Madden Inc.

Wolf Gordon

Designed by Patty Madden

BRW 9-2218   Tract

© Patty Madden Inc.

Wolf Gordon

Designed by Patty Madden

Summit
Textures

Mandarin
Vinyl Wallcovering
54" Wide

MRN 7-4755   Hong Kong

Wolf Gordon

Summit
Textures

VKY 7-4351   Fresh Mint

Wolf Gordon

Summit
Textures

Yutaka

Vinyl Wallcovering
54" Wide

YUT 7-4024   White Gold

Wolf Gordon

Summit
Textures

Florence
Vinyl Wallcovering
54" Wide

FLO 7-4100   Dapple

Wolf Gordon

Summit Textures

Bonaire
WALLCOVERING | Vinyl

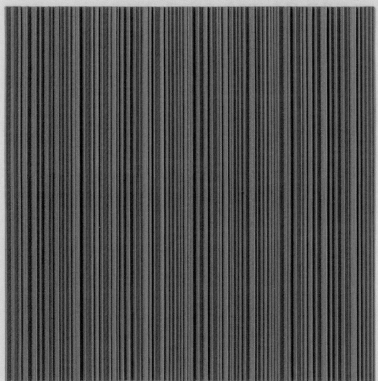

BNR 7-7762   Cement

Wolf Gordon

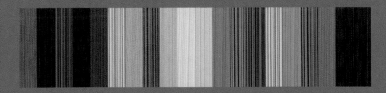

Textural Embosses 03

Shannon

Vinyl Wallcovering
52/54" Wide

785.17

VESCOM

Summit
Prints

Light

Vinyl Wallcovering
52/54" Wide

Designed by
Corinne Ulmann and Isamu Kanda

Surface over Structure:
Wolf-Gordon's Invitational
Design Competition
with the Students of the
Harvard GSD

LGT 7-3552   Ethereal

Wolf Gordon

Designed by Corinne Ulmann and Isamu Kanda

Summit
Prints

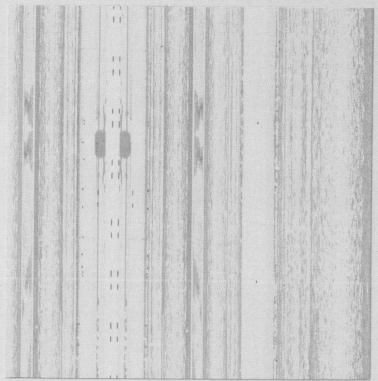

Transport

Vinyl Wallcovering
52/54" Wide

Designed by
Zac Culbreth

Surface over Structure:
Wolf-Gordon's Invitational
Design Competition
with the Students of the
Harvard GSD

TPT 7-3574   Viale

Wolf Gordon

Designed by Zac Culbreth

Kit of Parts

When you design with *Kit of Parts*, the final outcome is completely unique. The collection is comprised of two groupings of modular patterns — *City Series* and *Nature Series* — which give you the final word in creativity. You can choose from a range of palettes, mix and match an array of patterns and customize screen printed features. Try it out in our DesignLab at www.wolf-gordon.com/kitofparts.

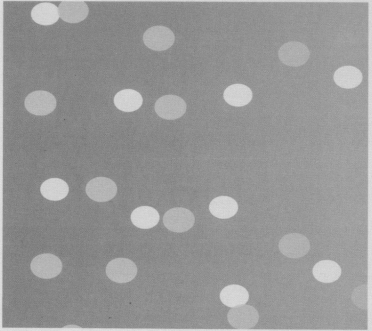

City Series, City Lights Fog

Wolf Gordon

Kit of Parts

Nature Series: Nature Tree, Nature Stripe, Nature Blossom

Wolf Gordon

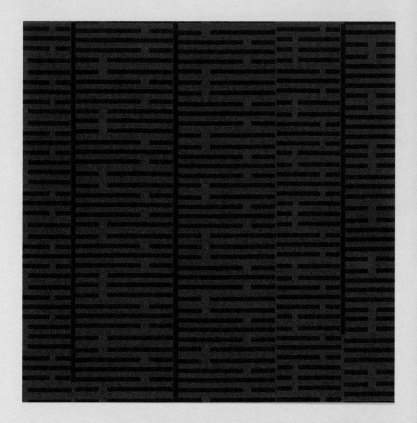

Summit
Prints

Rain Again
Vinyl Wallcovering
52/54" Wide

Designed by
Laurinda Spear

Wolf Gordon

Designed by Laurinda Spear

Summit
Prints

Noli
Vinyl Wallcovering
52/54" Wide

Designed by
Laurinda Spear

Wolf Gordon

Designed by Laurinda Spear

London Chic

Camden Passage

Vinyl Wallcovering
52" and 26" widths

Wolf Gordon

London Chic

Kensington

Vinyl Wallcovering
54" and 27" widths

Wolf Gordon

Metropolitan

High Line

HIGH PERFORMANCE UPHOLSTERY | Polyester/Cotton/Rayon

HLN 6564   Tulip

Wolf Gordon

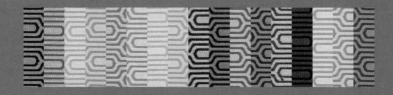

GRAPHICS AND BRANDING

Since 1967, the most consistent and character-laden aspect of our graphic identity has been the use of a wolf icon. Employing a figurative icon as part of a commercial logo dates to nineteenth-century France and the dawn of the advertising age; the Michelin Man is a prime example. Wolf-Gordon's wolf, changing form through the years, has remained an approachable, recognizable icon that is consistent with the company's spirit.

Theorists on branding claim that a brand's image can evolve depending on how it is positioned to achieve year-to-year business goals but that a brand's essence endures. It is the soul, the DNA, of the company. Even as Wolf-Gordon has grown and changed, with an ever more robust focus on design, we feel it is important to stay connected to our origins, which include honest business conduct, hard work, humor, and a bit of risk. This attitude must be manifest in our graphic identity as well as in undertakings across the organization.

As various graphic designers have taken on the challenge to update Wolf-Gordon's identity system, they have encountered a multifaceted company that defies easy categorization. While the sophisticated typographic treatments and functional color palettes of our identity system have changed over time, the wolf icon is a steadfast symbol that accepts and even encourages interpretation and transformation.

Graphic Identities, 1967–1997

The unknown author of our first logo deftly incorporated the letters W and G into the outline of a wolf's head. Later logos singled out the company name in typography and colors that were representative of their time. In 1997, we briefly resurrected the first wolf head logo while we worked on a more elaborate graphic identity system. Rick Wolf and David Gordon, the second generation of company management, called for a new branding strategy that embodied the energy they had assembled in a new executive team.

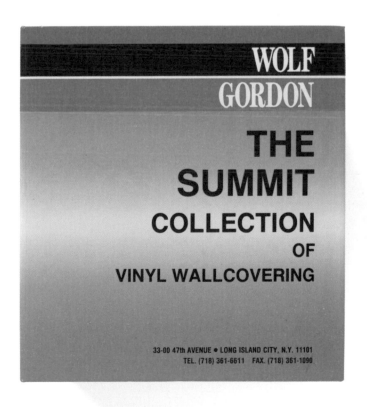

WOLF-GORDON
WALLCOVERINGS INC.

The Daytona Beach
Collection

of Vinyl Wallcoverings

132 WEST 21st STREET, NEW YORK, N.Y. 10011 (212) 255-3300

WOLF
GORDON

THE
SUMMIT
COLLECTION
OF
VINYL WALLCOVERING

33-00 47th AVENUE ● LONG ISLAND CITY, N.Y. 11101
TEL. (718) 361-6611   FAX. (718) 361-1090

Graphic Identity, 1998

Anthony Russell of Russell Design Associates developed a bold new logo to reflect our growth and evolution. His black-and-white mark was accompanied by an ever-changing cast of wolf silhouettes, from leaping King to baying Lowe. Strong shades of red, blue, and gold and three weights of Futura defined our stationery, catalog binders, and other printed pieces. Youthful, friendly, and flexible, the new identity system adapted easily to diverse items.

King
Letterhead; Second Sheet
Business Cards: National Sales Managers

Lillian
Envelope #10
Press Release
Business Card: Staff

Gregory
Business Card: Staff

Lupo
Mailing Label

Igor
Business Cards: Sales Representatives

Natasha
Business Cards: Executive Management

Wolf Cubs
Personnel Announcement
Business Cards: Creative Director

Borders catalog, wallcovering yardage calculator, designed by AHOY Studios

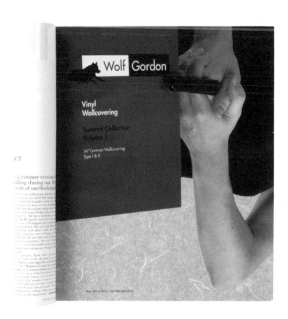

Graphic Variations, 1999, 2003

A successful graphic identity system must be as flexible as it is distinctive. Designer David Shields used the standards established by Anthony Russell in a binder cover cleverly co-branded for Wolf-Gordon and Dutch wallcovering company Vescom. The perforated grid is both eye-catching and ergonomic. AHOY Studios founders Aline Ozkan and Connie Koch have created numerous pieces for us, including a riveted brochure for digital printed wallcovering. Quotes and photographed vignettes inspired designers to delve into custom, site-specific installations.

Have you imagined the possibilities...

...of custom digital printed wallcovering?

supergraphics

"The great thing about being an architect is that you can walk into your dreams."

Harold E. Wagoner, Architect

photo collage

"Luck is the residue of design."

Holiday Card Calendars, 2001–2006

At Wolf-Gordon, we salute the holiday season with a special printed greeting. In the early 2000s, these were realized in a series of much anticipated calendars. The elaborately designed pieces were small enough to be pinned to a wall in a designer's workspace. Among the clever themes were phases of the moon and wild wolves, by AHOY Studios, and Wolf-Gordon-patterned origami and wolf adages, by Shaw Jelveh Design.

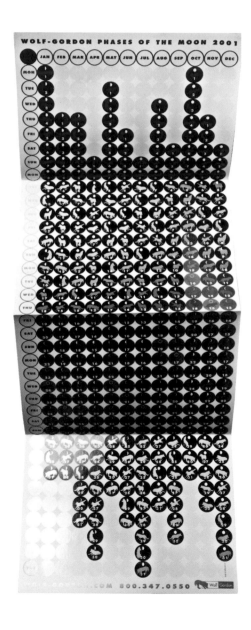

Advertisements, 2002–2003

To launch five collections—Digital Nature by Karim Rashid, the Premier Collection, the Suite Collection, EverSuede, and Touch by Petra Blaisse—we asked Stefan Sagmeister to create a series of print advertisements. Sagmeister, known for his unorthodox, provocative compositions, created typographic studies that interpreted each collection. For the Premier Collection, for example, he rendered the name in dried plant material, referencing the natural grasscloth and raffia components of the wallcoverings.

PREMIER III | NATURALS AND WOVENS | CONTRACT WALLCOVERINGS WWW.WOLF-GORDON.COM | 800 347 0550 | Wolf Gordon

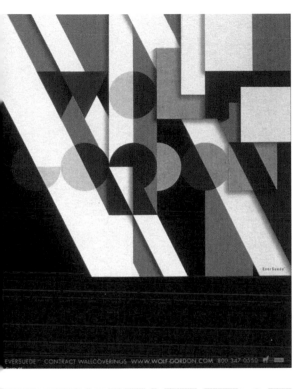

Advertisements, 2003–2008

Among the lengthy list of graphic materials developed by AHOY Studios was a memorable ad campaign based on Anthony Russell's wolf silhouettes. In upbeat vignettes of various commercial settings, from retail outlets to corporate offices, the designers set the shadows of human models side by side with wolves' shadows. The strong graphic content of these ads, which ran for several years, provided an interesting counterpoint to the featured wallcovering designs.

Lane 7, University Place, New York, 9:52 pm

Wolf Gordon

WOLF-GORDON VESCOM COLLECTION
PATTERN: SHANNON 9427.2 (shown at 100%)
800.347.0550 www.wolf-gordon.com

Piano Showroom, Los Angeles, 12:45 pm

Lobby, Mercer Street, New York, 2:15 pm

Department Store, North Michigan Avenue, Chicago 12:45 pm

Wolf Gordon

2nd Floor, Charleston Harbor, 9:37pm

Wolf Gordon

Graphic Identity, 2007

We began working with New York graphic designers 2x4 in 1999 on a capabilities brochure, the campaign for Linework by Laurinda Spear, and a website. In 2007, the firm, with partner Susan Sellers in the lead, revisited Wolf-Gordon's identity. The wolf silhouettes were consolidated into a singular, sharply angled form, and two shades of teal replaced the primary colors for stationery and other documents. Narrow stripes of bright colors—red for vinyl wallcovering, for instance—differentiated our catalogs by product category.

Wolf Gordon

Graphic Identity, 2013

Hjalti Karlsson and Jan Wilker of karlssonwilker formulated the next iteration of our identity. The partners kept the wolf, refined the typography, and specified a standout shade of "Yves Klein" blue. Ample white space, expanses of the vibrant new HKS 43 blue, and five weights of the Maison Neue typeface characterize all of our sales, communications, and product-related pieces. Our partnership with karlssonwilker extends far beyond the identity to include web design, advertising, work on our NeoCon sculptures and trade show booths, and myriad other projects we dream up.

Wolf Gordon

Rick Wolf

President
rick.wolf@wolfgordon.com

33-00 47th Avenue
Long Island City, NY 11101

800 347 0550 x415
Direct 718 391 5415

Wolf Gordon

HKS 43

Website, 2014

The Wolf-Gordon color spectrum is a key element in our graphic identity. Devised by karlssonwilker to highlight our vivid palette and variety of patterning, the color array comes to the fore in our website home page and product search. In fact, the innovative navigation is wholly generated by Wolf-Gordon wallcoverings, upholstery, and drapery textiles. Just as designers lay out samples on a tabletop to compare color and pattern, our website allows users to browse left and right through a selection of products. A tremendous depth of information on each item is just two clicks away.

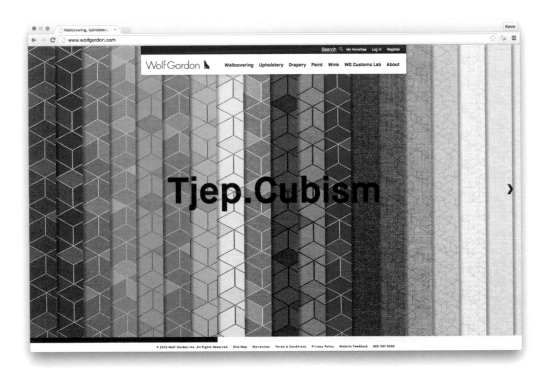

AD SCULPTURES

Each year, starting in January, we begin a twelve-month advertising and communications campaign that centers on the design process and installation of an air-borne sculpture. These works, presented at the Merchandise Mart in Chicago during NeoCon, our industry's most important trade show, draw on the creative, coordinating, engineering, and fabricating talents of a large team, including Wolf-Gordon marketing and design, karlssonwilker, The Guild (2012–2014), and AV&C (2015). Typically, the sculptures are twenty-six feet long by fourteen feet high and weigh up to 1,300 pounds. Suspended above an escalator between the first and second floors, the dimensional works transcend typical product display, transforming perceptions of the scope and diversity of our line. Each year the sculptures greet NeoCon attendees with a visually and spatially compelling fusion of art, design, product, and good will.

Before, during, and after NeoCon, we use the sculptures as the unifying theme for a year of print ads. We start the design process for the sculptures in November; our January ads present a simple sketch of the nascent piece. By March, the ads have progressed to confident, 3-D depictions that "lift off the page" via shadows and dimensional form. The May ads portray the fully articulated sculpture within a line drawing of the site at the Merchandise Mart. During the week of installation, we take a series of photos of the overall form in its space as well as details from various angles. The ads we place for the remainder of the year focus on these close-up images, completing the annual cycle of creation and celebration.

The Crystalline Dragon

We started the design process for our first sculpture with a clear idea of what we wanted to create: a multifaceted, energetic, asymmetric form inspired by both Bruno Taut's Glass Pavilion at the 1914 Cologne Werkbund exhibition and the pop-up retail phenomenon. It manifested the expansion of our product line into upholstery and drapery textiles via 250+ faceted panels, each cut and folded to the maximum yield of four-by-eight-foot sheets of substrate. This space-capturing, swooping form emphasized structure, color, and pattern.

ESCALATOR TO
SECOND LEVEL SHOPS
CTA RAPID TRANSIT STATION
THE MART FOOD COURT
McDONALD'S
→

175

177

Force of Nature

The 2013 sculpture embodied a serial repetition of rectangular form that grew out of our website and product photography formats. "Force of Nature" became a continuous barrel roll thanks to specially engineered "vertebrae" between each of the seventy twelve-by-ninety-six-inch panels. These uniform, rectangular box frames were slightly tapered on one side to create the gradual roll. We likened the effect to a powerful, abstracted animal spine.

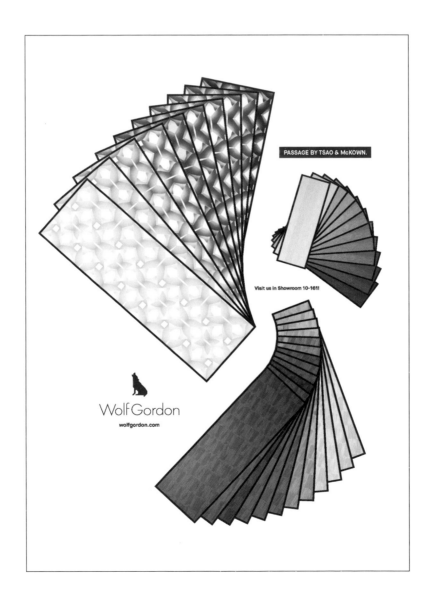

PASSAGE BY TSAO & McKOWN.

Visit us in Showroom 10-161!

WolfGordon
wolfgordon.com

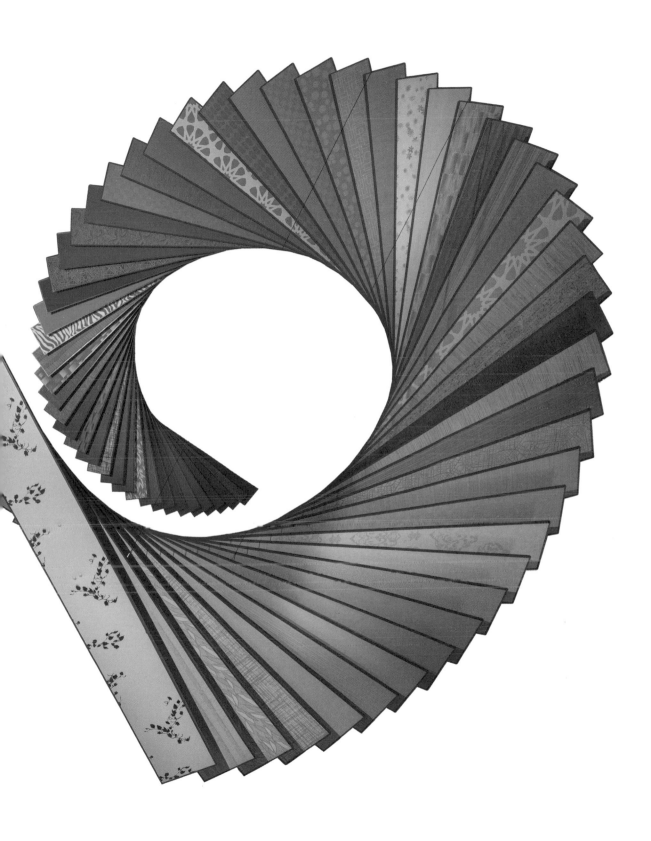

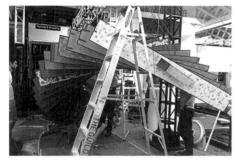

Wolf Gordon

Welcome to NeoCon 2013

Visit us in Showroom 10-161!

WolfGordon

The Ribbon Cloud

The year 2014 saw a transition from mineral and animal to organic and curvilinear. The Miró-esque piece featured twelve twelve-foot "ribbons"; while intertwined for visual complexity, each one curved to an identical radius. This assemblage was covered in 144 pieces of color-sorted wallcoverings and textiles.

189

SLICE

In 2015, inspired by the idea of interaction between escalator rider and sculpture, SLICE consisted of thirty-foot-long asymmetrical "winged" panels clad in more than fifteen thousand LEDs. Hidden in the panels were cameras that took and then transformed images of NeoCon attendees, morphing them into a unique, ever-evolving visualization. The first of our Ad Sculptures to use technology so explicitly, SLICE generated a grid of color fields so enticing that we used them for a digital wallcovering.

Toll, TLL 9-5313

Wall, WID 9-5330

Overpass, OVR 1445

Aidon, AID 1421

Aidon, AID 1425

Visit us at the new
wolfgordon.com

Wolf Gordon

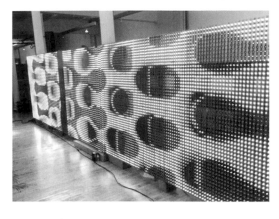

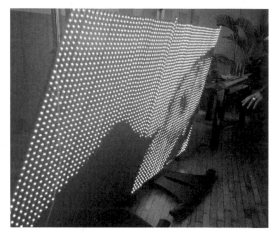

193

London Chic
wallcoverings

Wolf Gordon
www.wolfgordon.com

Wolf Gordon
www.wolfgordon.com

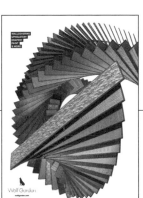

WALLCOVERING
UPHOLSTERY
DRAPERY
PAINT
& MORE

Wolf Gordon
wolfgordon.com

WALLCOVERING
UPHOLSTERY
DRAPERY
PAINT
& MORE

Wolf Gordon
wolfgordon.com

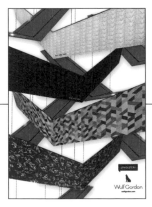

WG
Customs
Lab

Wolf Gordon
wolfgordon.com

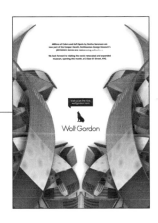

Visit us at the Fair.
wolfgordon.com

Wolf Gordon

UPHOLSTERY

Wolf Gordon
wolfgordon.com

Wolf Gordon
wolfgordon.com

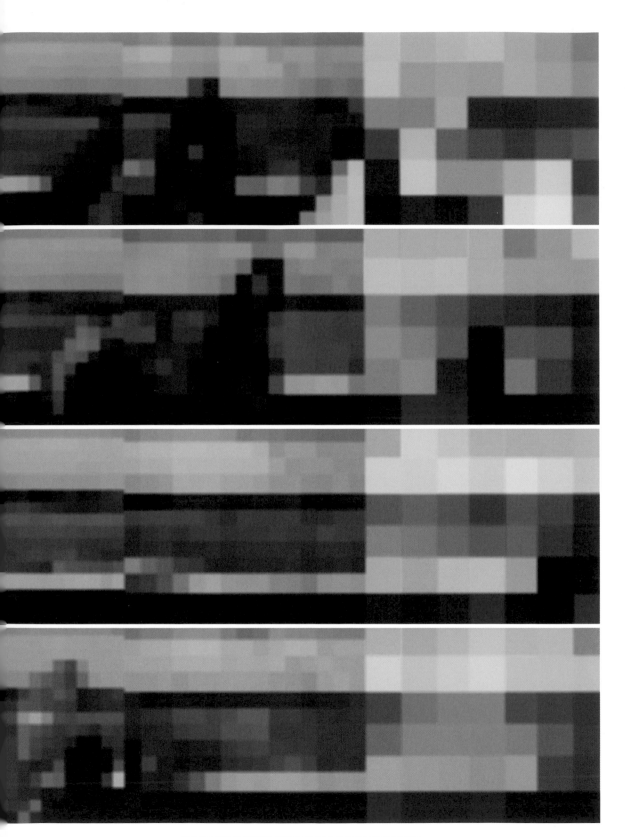

Progressive digitization of escalator passengers

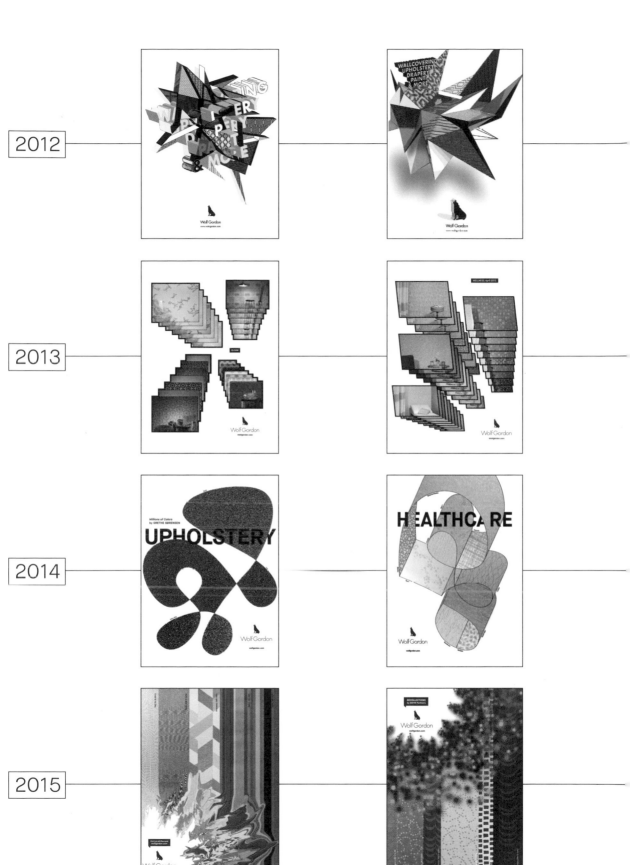

2012

2013

2014

2015

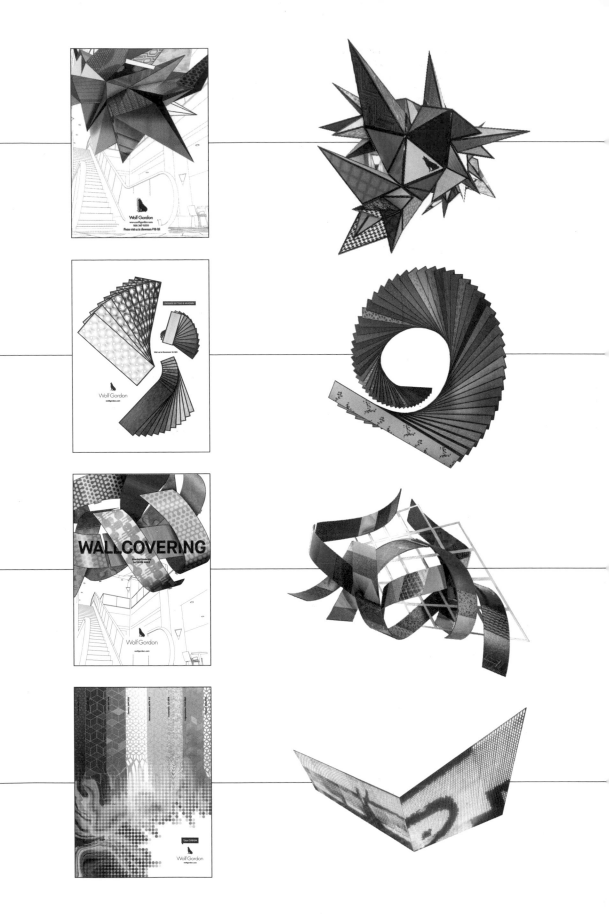

PRODUCTS
2012–2015

FLOWER by Tsao & McKown
Contract **Wallcovering**

800 347 0550
wolfgordon.com

FWD 103 Bluet

Wolf Gordon ◤

Designed by Tsao & McKown

London Chic

Bankside

Vinyl Wallcovering
54" and 27" widths

Wolf Gordon

London Chic

Savile Row

Vinyl Wallcovering
54" and 27" widths

Wolf Gordon

Gleam

Silvia

WALLCOVERING | Vinyl

Wolf Gordon

Gleam

Alhambra
WALLCOVERING | Vinyl

Wolf Gordon

Gleam

Tivoli
WALLCOVERING | Vinyl

Wolf Gordon

Gleam

Handel
WALLCOVERING | Vinyl

Wolf Gordon

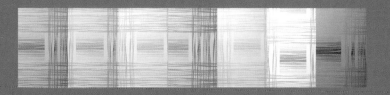

SOFT SPOTS by Grethe Sørensen
Contract **Wallcovering**

800 347 0550
wolfgordon.com

DSS 112 Spring

WolfGordon

Designed by Grethe Sørensen

Millions of Colors
High Performance Woven **Upholstery**
Designed by Grethe Sørensen

Grethe Sørensen has revolutionized the art of tapestry
by inventing a method to convert photographic
pixels into threads, marrying traditional methods of
craftsmanship to modern digital technology.

This textile has a very large repeat of 56" x 218", so each upholstered item will likely feature different areas of the pattern.

Wolf Gordon

Designed by Grethe Sørensen

Metropolitan

Harbor

HIGH PERFORMANCE, INDOOR/OUTDOOR UPHOLSTERY
Solution Dyed Polypropylene

bd Bella-Dura®
Beautiful. Durable. Back to Earth.

HAB 8206   Marine

Wolf Gordon

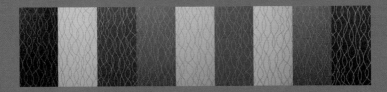

Metropolitan

Wander

HIGH PERFORMANCE, INDOOR/OUTDOOR UPHOLSTERY
Solution Dyed Polypropylene

bd Bella-Dura®
Beautiful. Durable. Back to Earth.

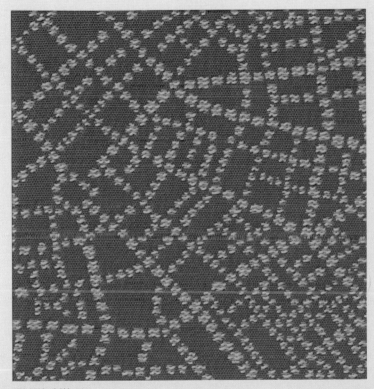

WDR 8009   Cobblestone

Wolf Gordon

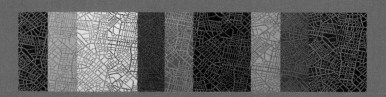

Tracking
High Performance Woven **Upholstery**

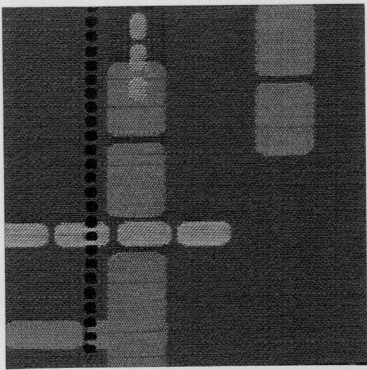

TRK 1335 Umber

WolfGordon

Inversion
High Performance Woven **Upholstery**

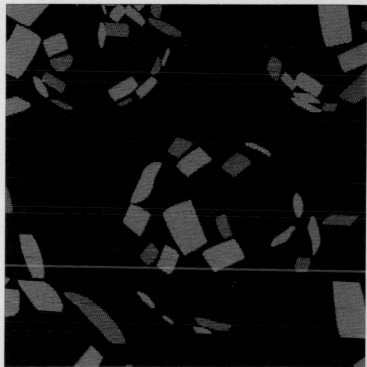

IVR 1350 Coal

WolfGordon ◣

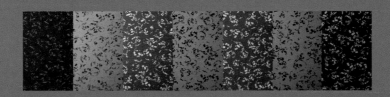

Gleam

Marz
Vinyl Wallcovering
Designed by Kevin Walz

Fine artist and designer Kevin Walz explores
two-sidedness in "Overlay/Underlay,"
a collection of wallcoverings that utilize
transparent inks to create patterns
with a dual vision.

© Kevin Walz

Wolf Gordon

Designed by Kevin Walz

Gleam

Honeykomb
Vinyl Wallcovering
Designed by Kevin Walz

Fine artist and designer Kevin Walz explores
two-sidedness in "Overlay/Underlay,"
a collection of wallcoverings that utilize
transparent inks to create patterns
with a dual vision.

© Kevin Walz

WolfGordon

Designed by Kevin Walz

Atlas
Contract **Wallcovering**

ATA 2066 Silver

Wolf Gordon

Ember
Contract **Wallcovering**

EBR 2237 Facade

Wolf Gordon ◣

Gleam

Wide

Vinyl **Wallcovering**

Designed by Morgan Bajardi

Morgan Bajardi engineers graphics to enhance the visual experience of pattern, integrating research, life experience, and the science of sight. Her roots as a textile designer are in San Francisco, Italy, India and London, where she completed her studies at Central Saint Martins at University of the Arts London.

Wolf Gordon

Designed by Morgan Bajardi

Gleam

Tall
Vinyl **Wallcovering**
Designed by Morgan Bajardi

Morgan Bajardi engineers graphics to enhance the visual experience of pattern, integrating research, life experience, and the science of sight. Her roots as a textile designer are in San Francisco, Italy, India and London, where she completed her studies at Central Saint Martins at University of the Arts London.

© Morgan Bajardi

Wolf Gordon

Designed by Morgan Bajardi

Designed by Boym Partners

Gleam

Broadway
Vinyl **Wallcovering**
Designed by Boym Partners

Partners in a New York-based design studio,
Constantin and Laurene Boym bring an
experimental approach to a collection of
wallcoverings, infused with their
illustrious humor and wit.

© Boym Partners

WolfGordon

Designed by Boym Partners

Gleam

Basis
Vinyl **Wallcovering**
Designed by Frank Tjepkema

Frank Tjepkema (born 1970) is a Dutch
designer based in Amsterdam. He started his
design agency Tjep. in 2001 and works in
interior design, architecture, product design,
visual design and jewellery.

Wolf Gordon

Designed by Frank Tjepkema

Gleam

Osmosis
Vinyl Wallcovering
Designed by Frank Tjepkema

Frank Tjepkema (born 1970) is a Dutch
designer based in Amsterdam. He started his
design agency Tjep. in 2001 and works in
interior design, architecture, product design,
visual design and jewellery.

Wolf Gordon

Designed by Frank Tjepkema

Overpass
High Performance Woven **Upholstery**

OVR 1440 Carmine

Wolf Gordon

OWN WORDS: AN ORAL HISTORY OF WOLF-GORDON

David Sokol

BERNIE GORDON
COFOUNDER

I knew Mel Wolf for eighty years. He came to Manhattan from Baltimore, and we met in the sixth grade. When we were still students, around 1946, he got me a job at Gilford, Inc., a textile company. We worked there for twenty years after the war.

In late 1966, Mr. Gilford told us that he was halving our salaries, effective immediately. He was seventy-two, and we found out later that he was trying to make the company more salable. Regardless, we weren't going to take this; we had six kids between us. So we may not have wanted to go into business, but four days after his announcement, we figured we'd better go into business.

We never thought Gilford would be in jeopardy. Mr. Gilford's suppliers were another matter: Mr. Gilford had no children, and they were concerned about the business if he were to die. So when we decided to launch our own company, the suppliers were thrilled to have these young people sell their products. In fact, one manufacturer had just moved to a factory in New Jersey and still had three years on a lease on Twenty-first Street. He gave us the space for half the rent. The sample book maker? He didn't ask for a nickel until we could pay him.

At the time, producing a sample book took seven months. Mel and I continued working at Gilford during this period, and the two top salesmen, Tony Prota and Frank Carr, figured something was up. When they finally asked us about it, they said they wanted in. On August 7, 1967, Mel and I walked into Mr. Gilford's office and told him he could have his business. And it's no wonder he didn't have a heart attack, because five minutes later, Frank and Tony quit, too.

Within half an hour of walking into our new office on Twenty-first Street, we were calling customers. My wife, Reva, came to work as the telephone operator, and Mel's wife, Dotty, was the bookkeeper.

Back then, practically nobody was using vinyl as wallcovering. It was really new. Architects and interior designers were thrilled to see it in a sample book, because they wanted something that could stand up to abuse by stockbrokers and hospital workers. If you put it on the wall, you wouldn't have to touch it for ten years; whereas with paint, every two or three years you'd have to take a room out of use for upkeep. End users didn't want to be bothered with that.

For many years, in our business you ordered from a sample book, we phoned the mill, and the mill shipped it. Our only inventory was returns. I personally was never in favor of putting things in stock. Our biggest problem was that our reps could work for a year getting one of our products specified, and then a local distributor who had access to the same lines could go in and get the order by undercutting us on price.

DAVID GORDON
EXECUTIVE VP

I used to work summers—in the shipping department, as a messenger—I did a bit of everything. When I graduated from college in 1976, my father said, "Why don't you try working here full time?" I worked from the bottom up, starting in the order department, spending a number of years in customer service, going out to see clients, and overseeing the complaint department. Once you learn how to handle complaints, you can handle anything.

Back then, since our parents didn't believe in inventory, we had a hard time distinguishing our products out in the field. And because of our limited national sales force, we had problems obtaining exclusive territories to represent a factory's product lines. When our parents retired, we needed to be more competitive and more proprietary with all our designs. To do this we did two things. The first was to start creating and manufacturing exclusive patterns. The second was to expand our sales force around the country so we could start to represent mills' exclusive products in certain areas. We negotiated the exclusive rights to represent Vescom nationally and J. Josephson in a large part of the United States.

RICK WOLF

PRESIDENT AND CEO

While I was in college, I always thought I would work for IBM, because I liked programming. But it was a bad economy in 1982, and my father was dying for one of his children to go into the business. So I figured I would give it a shot. David was in customer service at the time, and we both worked in that department my first year.

BERNIE GORDON

When we started this company, Mel and I were 40 percent partners, and Frank and Tony each owned 10 percent. Because Frank and Tony were a good decade younger than the two of us, we thought the business would go to them, not to our kids. Unfortunately, both of them died, both at sixty-three, and Mel and I bought out their shares. I retired in 1991 at sixty-seven, but Mel? He said, "They'll have to carry me out of here." A few years later he had his first stroke, so he only stayed on until 1995. But for the next fifteen years of his life, I never saw a guy who had it so tough be so cheerful.

I'm proud of what we did when we were running the place, and I'm proud of the natural evolution that has taken place at the company since then. In order to stay in business, you have to keep coming up with new things, and that's why Wolf-Gordon now commits so many resources to design, for example. I have a different opinion about inventory than David and Rick, but the ratio of sales to inventory is comparable to what it was in my day. To be as big as the company is, the right decisions are being made.

RICK WOLF

There's no doubt my father and Bernie did a great job. But we were rudderless in the period between 1985 and 1995. At the time I thought I just didn't yet understand the industry; still, we were flat while other companies were growing, and we weren't doing anything to change that. Around the time Bernie retired in 1991,

my brother Rob and I flew to Santa Fe to put together a business plan with our oldest brother, Larry. It showed that our business had shrunk relative to inflation. Every change we've made since then was anticipated in that business plan, whether we referred to it or not.

ROB WOLF

CFO

I started at Wolf-Gordon in 1986. At the time we really couldn't do anything to change or grow the business, because our parents and their associates owned and ran the company. So we decided that even if we couldn't implement anything, we should at least create a business plan. It was part of something bigger that Rick and I discussed. We said to ourselves, It doesn't really matter if we don't know what we're doing as we try to grow the business, as long as we're trying to do something. We were trying to be more creative—we developed a new computer system, we made that business plan with the help of our brother Larry. Even though we didn't know exactly what to do, we just couldn't do what the company had always done. We at least needed to put energy into change.

RICK WOLF

A real turning point came in the early nineties. Frank Carr was friendly with Patty Madden, and in the eighties she had created two series of Metropole for Wolf-Gordon. This was a vinyl wallcovering that our customers could customize with screen printing. Patty felt she could bring a new vision to the wallcovering industry, and because of Metropole, she spoke to us about that vision first. But we still hadn't changed our position on inventory, so Patty went over to JM Lynne, which was interested in those new, exclusive types of wallcovering, and she really put them on the map. It was something of a wake-up call, though we couldn't do much until my father retired.

PATTY MADDEN
DESIGNER

Wolf-Gordon gave me my first opportunity with Metropole. I was working for a company called Walker Group, which did all the design for retailers like Burdines. I had to design product for these stores because we were looking for wallcoverings and fabrics that were super-contemporary. There was nothing available, so I would sit on a light box and paint designs on fabrics and wallcoverings. We knew we could get them made because we had a tremendous amount of yardage. I would give the designs to Frank Carr, and Wolf-Gordon would do a custom job. After a while, Frank said, "Why don't we do a collection?" He posed it to Bernie and Mel, and that's how Metropole started. It's kind of how I got into this business.

They're really good people at Wolf-Gordon. In the early nineties, when I wanted to develop new products, I went to them first. David and Rick wanted to go for it, but their fathers didn't. I made the collection with JM Lynne instead, and it caught fire. At that point the market was mainly Buccaneer Suede and stipples—neutrals and textures were pretty much all that was out there, and everybody had the same thing. It was nice to come out with something unique, to bring real design and color to vinyl.

ROB WOLF

Our revenue went down between 1994 and 1995, which was unnerving. I was dating someone at the time, and we both had children. I remember that she expressed concern about my ability to support the kids.

DAVID GORDON

After Mel retired, and seeing JM Lynne's success with Patty, we decided to start creating our own patterns. I worked with stylists on two of our initial converted collections, Circa and Translations. Back in the early nineties, the philosophy of the interior designers was to keep the wall decoration simple. They would choose the carpet and furniture first and then let the walls complement and not clash with all their furnishings. This philosophy helped us determine that the patterns in our first collections should be conservative and small-scale. Natural looks and faux stones dominated.

During those early years some of our most successful patterns were imitation vinyl suedes that had a nice mottled effect. Imitation fabrics, like rice paper and silk, followed. While a designer has the ability to create exciting wallcoverings, it may not always make sense to invest in that creativity. First, it is sometimes hard to visualize what the wallcovering will look like on the wall from seeing it in the catalog, and second, the designs might be too specific to coexist with the other elements in the room.

RICK WOLF

Although we began taking an inventory position with some new products, we didn't yet understand how to design well. It's important in business to hire the right people to take on a challenge, and then let them find their way. That was our answer to making our own designs.

Before we could embrace that change, though, we wanted to create a new sales manager position. Most everyone recommended Mike Gorelick and Mark Mendlen as the best in the field. They were at Maharam. I remember calling up Mike, and he thought I was my father—what I mean is that he thought we were a stodgy company that was not design-oriented, that we just flipped through sample books with clients. Mike never would have come over if it weren't for Mark, because it was Mark who saw the big picture—that the company in its current state offered a real opportunity. They decided to come over as a team in May of 1997. Around the same time Scuffmaster came to us to distribute its paint, and there was great motivation to do it in spite of the costs, like educating our sales force and certifying installers—this was another unique product that would help us move into the next chapter of growth.

DAVID GORDON

With Scuffmaster, I saw an opportunity to broaden our line. Compared to wallcovering, paint has always been a much bigger market, and this gave us an opportunity to get into a boutique, high-end paint product that did not compete with the patterns and textures in our existing lineup of wallcoverings. In addition to increasing revenue, Scuffmaster paint helped us to enhance our exposure as a company.

MIKE GORELICK
VP OF SALES

At first I had no interest in joining Wolf-Gordon, and it was Mark who gnawed away at me. He kept saying that the company's current condition was good for us—that we could get a run going.

A run means your sales go way up several years in a row. You reach a whole new plateau of sales income—and maybe, a new perception as a brand. Starting a run is a formula. The first rule is to assemble a bunch of talented performers, not just businesspeople carrying suitcases. In that first year or two, we got rid of all of the independent sales representatives. We added cool, interesting, creative performers to the team, and we gave them presentation kits and sample bags and showed them how to use them.

That's all we did, but we were written up by some trade publication for all the new patterns we had introduced! The reality is we hadn't introduced a single thing. We just re-packaged and re-presented what we had. I used to be a magician, and that translated perfectly to sales.

The formula isn't based on having the best product; it's based on selling. But if you can take the selling engine and really refine it and grow it and get it purring, and then bring in somebody like Marybeth and do both great sales and great design, then you can create the run as well as the perfect storm.

MARYBETH SHAW
VP OF DESIGN AND MARKETING

In the summer of 1997, I had just left my job with an architecture firm for freelance design work. A headhunter called me about a position at this wallpaper company in Queens, and I went and met with Liana Toscanini, who had been helping Rick with some marketing over the previous year. When I received the job description, I asked Rick if he would mind my rewriting the position as creative director so I could list all the things I wanted to bring to the table.

I just couldn't resist redefining the position. Wolf-Gordon, at the time, was like a completely malleable object. It needed a major overhaul, but there was an infusion of energy with Mike and Mark on board. It was a fun venture to turn this ship around and to be entrepreneurial.

I started in late August, and within a week, we embarked on a complete rethinking of our booth for the October Interplan trade show at the Javits Center. If we were going to attract attention and have any kind of success, the booth needed to have an architecturally informed quality. I asked architect Ali Tayar to design the booth for us, and Desai/Chia Architecture executed the scheme. I also took our graphic identity to a friend, Aline Ozkan, who reworked a wolf-head brandmark that the company had used as its logo in the late 1960s. Internally, the company had never experienced anything like this kind of work.

It took me longer to have an impact on product. In 1997, at the recommendation of our Los Angeles sales representative Ronni Massok, we were producing two popular patterns: an imitation figured maple called Alpine and an imitation rice paper called Jasmine. I felt strongly that we needed to go beyond the world of wallcovering stylists and work with designers from other fields to bring fresh concepts to our patterning. Susan Grant Lewin suggested I speak with architect Laurinda Spear in 1999. Laurinda had, at that time, started to apply her very distinctive graphic and color sense to products.

LAURINDA SPEAR
FOUNDING PRINCIPAL OF ARQUITECTONICA

People really experience a building at the small scale. They don't experience it as an elevation, or from a bird's-eye perspective. They use a building in the details, and those details shouldn't become unsatisfying. It is those little things that keep a building with bravado on the outside from being ho-hum on the inside. That's why we're interested in designing at all scales. Wallcovering was a natural step.

Marybeth is a wonderful client—she's a designer, she has great ideas. And Rick and David trust her implicitly. They didn't give us a strict design brief. They simply asked, "What are you thinking about? What would you specify?" So we brought in stacks and stacks and stacks of boards and put them all over the New York showroom. There were easily a hundred designs there, and David, Rick, and Marybeth reviewed them all. We didn't always see eye to eye about the scale of pattern, but they know their market and they wanted a collection that would sell. Also, we tried to make something that other architects could specify, something with universal appeal that wasn't so idiosyncratic to us.

MARYBETH SHAW

Laurinda's collection could have been done in nine months start to finish, but I had a lot of convincing to do. When Linework finally did come out in 2001, it stimulated very strong reactions for and against. To me, this was a success—it lodged in people's memories. The graphic sensibility and color saturation were so different from the watered-down, layered inks that were dominating commercial wallcovering at the time. Linework was a shock to everyone's sensibility, and I'm happy that we made such an impact with it. It was published all over the world.

MIKE GORELICK

The reps, and even Mark and me, didn't get it. We didn't know who would use Laurinda's designs. But Rick kept telling us, "Most people don't get the art that hangs in a museum." What was important was that Linework got us noticed as a forward-thinking, creative group. It changed the mindset.

The product that sells versus the product that attracts attention—they're two completely different things. But the product that attracts attention is worth an investment in advertising many times over. While we did mostly continue selling staples, as the products got more interesting, our salespeople had more of a dialogue to sell everything.

MARYBETH SHAW

We followed up on Linework with Digital Nature by Karim Rashid; Touch by Petra Blaisse was also in the works. Designtex then purchased JM Lynne, which freed up Patty Madden to work with us again. She developed a fresh new micro-engraving process, and she did an increased number of colorways for each pattern. Her lines became extremely popular.

PATTY MADDEN

When JM Lynne was sold, I still did products for them, but I was pretty much free to work for whomever. And of course I was very eager to do products with Wolf-Gordon, coming full circle after so many years. I was so excited to see the transformation in the company—that made me really happy.

There were certain technical things I was doing, certain types of embossing, that were exclusive to me. I also had been doing a lot of hospitality, and so I knew that market pretty well. Wolf-Gordon wanted as much product as they could get. It was a wonderful, creative time; we were combining unique design with technology that had never been used before. The team was great to work with, and the salespeople were extremely enthusiastic.

One book, called Etchings, was a nice combination of patterns and stripes and leaves—at the time people wanted a lot of coordinates. Of course, it was nice to sell product and make money, but as an artist, it's about seeing that what you do makes a difference. I was amazed at all the times I'd walk into an interior and the product would be there.

RICK WOLF

The perception of Wolf-Gordon was changing, though business remained flat after 9/11. We really started turning a profit in 2003. Patty's work helped us take off and helped us increase our presence in hospitality. For years after 2003, we were growing at 20 percent annually.

MARYBETH SHAW

I moved to Baltimore in 2002, and continued to work for Wolf-Gordon through December 2003, but it was challenging to manage marketing and special collections from a distance. It felt like the right time to build my own design practice, Shaw Jelveh Design.

Kari Pei did interesting work at Wolf-Gordon after I left. Kari was committed to sustainability, for example—she introduced a product line called Organics, which was completely biodegradable. She also grew our custom design department through hospitality commissions, and she conducted the Surface Over Structure program at the Harvard Graduate School of Design, which was a good example of private industry pairing with academia on a real, manufactured product.

ABBY SUCKLE
ARCHITECT

Kari and I started collaborating with GSD alumni on a competition for renovations to the guest rooms at the Harvard Club, which was supposed to be an opportunity for recent graduates to get a design constructed. I was on the Art and Architecture Committee of the Harvard Club and brought Kari in to talk about how to use wallcovering.

She and I went out to dinner and talked about how architecture students never really go through the whole construction process, because the semester is very short and they never get beyond the concept phase. Kari said that wallcovering could be very quick, and that it could be possible to have students experience manufacturing.

CORINNE ULMANN
WINNER OF SURFACE OVER
STRUCTURE WITH ISAMU KANDA

Realizing our design from concept to final production on such a short timeline was a gift from Wolf-Gordon, especially considering that the building process often takes years. It makes sense for companies like Wolf-Gordon to engage with students to tap innovation, since the practical realities of a large company may not be able to support sustained exploration.

MIKE GORELICK

Marybeth left too soon. She didn't see the fruits of her labor, because our industry works in arrears. Starting in the financial crisis and economic downturn in 2007–8, we examined everything. The thing that was missing? We had gone on autopilot in marketing and design. Rick felt that that had to be reinvented, like it was before. "Let's get Marybeth back in here," he said. "Let's get attention and notice for creative and cool things, and let's do this again."

MARYBETH SHAW

It takes at least nine to twelve months to start selling a design, because that's how long it takes a designer to identify a pattern he or she has seen as appropriate for an upcoming project. A dramatically new design might not take off for a few years. Mike Gorelick calls this arrears.

ROB WOLF

Whether you're discussing our first big rebound with Mike and Mark, or our success with Patty Madden, or Marybeth coming back to the company, you get this sense that people have a lot of goodwill toward us and wanted to work with us even when we weren't at our strongest internally. I like to think that's because we treat employees compassionately, we're cohesive, and we let people be what they want to be. You don't feel autocracy or bureaucracy here. You have voice and expression, and that should inspire you to pursue a vision.

MARYBETH SHAW

My second tenure with Wolf-Gordon, heading up both product design and marketing, began in September 2011. It's important to note that I was coming back to a company that, in addition to selling wallcovering, was beginning to offer upholstery and drapery textiles with new features, qualities, and performance, as well as Wink, the first clear dry-erase coating offered for commercial interiors.

RICK WOLF

We had offered upholstery at one point in the past, but the supplier was undependable. The Dutch company Vescom had developed a line that it was selling in Europe—it also bought some European manufacturers of mohairs and wovens—and it wanted us to distribute these lines in the United States. We felt that would be a good first step for us because we'd have a fairly large line to launch with and then expand that offering with our own products. This was an opportunity that came to us, and we knew we could build on it strategically. We also knew, frankly, that upholstery holds clients' attention more—people examine samples with their eyes and hands, whereas you don't really feel obliged to feel a wallcovering sample. Being more of a one-stop source for designers was intriguing, and it allowed us not just to grow our market share but to go into an altogether new market.

MARYBETH SHAW

Moving into upholstery and drapery was a huge endeavor for Wolf-Gordon. We needed to get up to speed on the special features of textiles, and to educate our sales force and gradually convince our customers that they could trust us to design and deliver top-quality commercial upholstery and drapery. Ultimately, I believe developing both wallcoverings and textiles has made us stronger in both categories. Wink also permitted us to be at the forefront of flexible, highly functional workspace design.

HJALTI KARLSSON
COFOUNDER OF KARLSSONWILKER

It's quite clear that Marybeth came back to Wolf-Gordon with a mission to take the company to a certain place. When we first started working together, initially to create an experience at the Merchandise Mart for NeoCon, she and I went to Chicago to survey the building for different installation locations. We looked at four or five spots, and Marybeth focused on pretty much the craziest one—the air space above a prominent escalator. Even the building had never used it for that purpose.

JAN WILKER
COFOUNDER OF KARLSSONWILKER

Marybeth wanted to do something big, certainly not something ordinary. She also wanted to create an ad campaign that would build up to the NeoCon installation, revealing the process of how we got there. The campaign went step by step: every ad showed our latest creative development, and photography of the final installation made up the last ads of the year. Breaking open the process like that—not just showing shots of product with a logo—it was a much bigger concept.

After that, we worked toward developing a more holistic identity for Wolf-Gordon, one with more energy and optimism. It needed to communicate that it was fun to work at Wolf-Gordon, and fun to design space; that it was possible to be positive without sacrificing the quality and sincerity and care of the company.

The relationship is very close. We're a small studio, and Marybeth is always on hand; this is not a corporate structure where people can hide. There are times when we push Wolf-Gordon creatively, and times when they push us. Not just Marybeth, but the whole company. They really seem to trust us, which is important—otherwise we couldn't do any of the things we do. And in that way Wolf-Gordon was a first for our studio. They allowed us to reposition them and create their new identity. They were open to it and ready for it, and we got to move their soul.

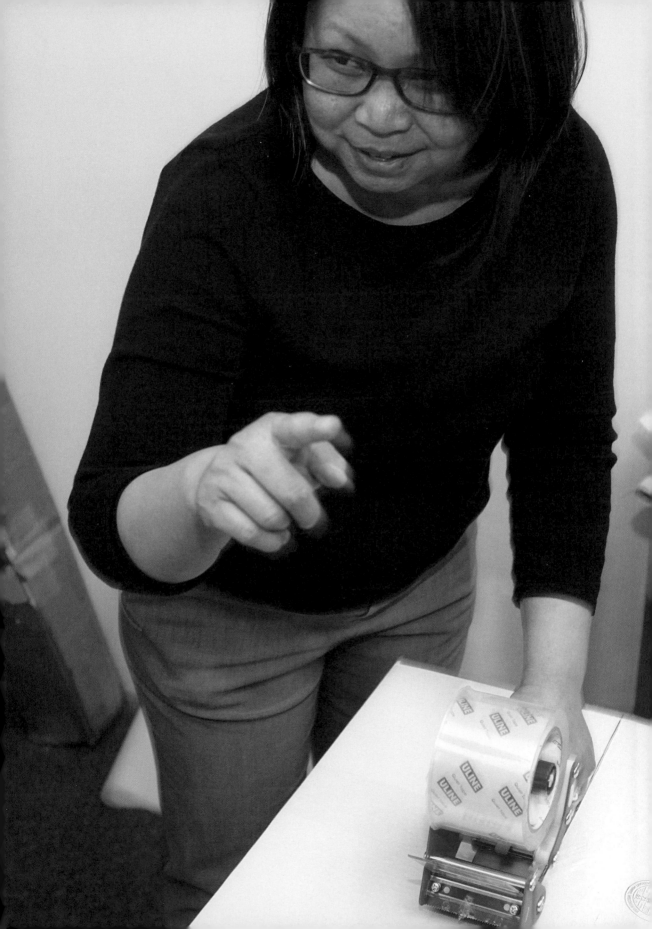

HJALTI KARLSSON

We're proud of the whole body of work, plus the fact that we continue to work together. I hope someone who looks at the ad campaigns and NeoCon sculptures and the overall identity would be able to understand that Wolf-Gordon product occupies the same realm. I hope they'll get excited about the product itself, and see Wolf-Gordon as an energetic company that's curious about new things and wants to try new things.

MARYBETH SHAW

When I came back to Wolf-Gordon in 2011, I was in a position to establish sustainability policy. With Shaw Jelveh Design, I had become familiar with the green building sector through work with the U.S. Green Building Council. I did more than eighty design projects for USGBC, so I brought that sense of responsibility back with me. In the last few years, the green building movement has begun focusing on products' impacts on human health. With our sustainability consultant YR&G as a guide, we started moving toward our current policy of transparency. As a result, we are the first and only commercial wallcovering company that has asked all of our partner mills to fill out our sustainability and LEED forms and to complete health product declarations.

In retrospect, I think my time away from Wolf-Gordon was positive because I was able to bring new skills back to the company, whether from the point of view of sustainability or simply managing people; and of course, I was happy to be back at the company, working with Rick and David, and in New York. Of all aspects of this work, I most love seeking out design talent internationally and curating the licensed design collections. Collaborating with designers like Petra Blaisse, Grethe Sørensen—really all of them— is a phenomenal and fulfilling experience. You get to know each other well through that shared process.

KEVIN WALZ

ARTIST AND DESIGNER
I started doing designs for Wolf-Gordon in

the summer of 2013, when I decided to move from Rome back to New York. For the previous two or three years I had been doing a series of paintings that addressed the canvas from both sides—with texture and color saturating through the material and affecting pattern on either side. When Marybeth contacted me and asked if there was a certain direction I wanted to pursue, this series immediately came to mind, and I told her I was interested in creating patterning that had layers and layers of texture.

Wolf-Gordon was supportive, and really interested in what I wanted to do. They listened and gave me a lot of technical support and made very positive suggestions. It was a project I could sink my teeth into, and I could try things that were kind of a throwback, because it's the opposite of computer-generated drawing. This project still encompassed technology, because we made gazillions of very big files to create these textures that couldn't have been created any other way, but we're not just doing programmed line weights. We're creating the opposite; we're creating static. It was a really fun project, and it was an exhausting project.

MARYBETH SHAW

Our product line is large enough to contain what design specifiers think they need, as well as the things they don't know they need. The acoustical drapery sheers that we introduced to the U.S. market in 2014, which came out of Vescom's research with designer Annette Douglas, is one example of staying ahead of demand. I'm also excited about the coming launch of Rampart: this is a high-performance wall protection product that has a super coating on it that resists scratching as well as a through-color and shallow emboss that hide blemishes on the wall. More generally speaking, we need to be proactive, and we do so by bringing all kinds of "outside voices" into our wall-covering community and by prioritizing design in product development.

DAVID GORDON

It's amazing how the 70-30 rule works. You really need 30 percent of your inventory to be great sellers. With the rest, you strike a balance between what will garner attention, the twenty colorways that may or may not be specified, and the really nice design that could be a home run.

You can't be scared to fail, though I would say we've done our best with tweaks. Going all the way back to those suedes: after years of selling it so well, we thought of coming out with embossed versions. That became one of our biggest sellers. Sometimes design energy is devoted to making an existing product better, or expanding it, or figuring out the next generation of it. How would I like it to go even further? I want to see wallcoverings and upholstery that offer functionality in addition to aesthetics—to have thermal mass, or offer to take your vital signs, or kill viruses.

RICK WOLF

When I walk into an interior with wall-covering, it feels so much better. I'm not advocating covering every wall, but if you walk into a hotel with bare walls, for example, you just don't have the same sense of welcome. Marybeth grasps this and conveys this notion in a much more romantic way. She has repositioned Wolf-Gordon from a company that sells design to a design company. I knew it was right, but it was also a battle. You just have to try. Otherwise, you're not growing.

MIKE GORELICK

Now the challenge is to get to that next level. When I started here, the face of Wolf-Gordon was a New York salesman—a salesman, not a saleswoman. It was a guy, older than the people he was calling on, wearing a trench coat and carrying a catalog. Clearly not a personal friend of the customer. I'm proudest of evolving us away from that identity, and I think having even more representatives who identify with our customers, and perhaps serve as icons for them, will take us to the next level. But you have to be a design

leader, in addition to a sales and customer service leader, in order to excel; all of that creativity and work has to have happened. To that end, I appreciate how David puts ideas to the test, and I feel secure in Marybeth's vision.

MARYBETH SHAW

I feel that as a company that markets and sells product to designers, we are obliged to participate with them in the design continuum—in pushing the discipline forward. If you're constantly in reactive mode, then you're just waiting to see what other companies are selling and coming out with your version of it, which is not really serving your audience. But if you're looking for concept-driven designers across disciplines and determining whose work might enhance wallcovering or upholstery or drapery, then the job becomes quite meaningful. It goes without saying that we enhance the quality of interior spaces with well-designed product. What sets us apart is how we go beyond well-designed product into an experimental and integrative visual culture.

CONTRIBUTORS

Melissa Feldman has worked as an art director and design writer/ editor for magazines, corporations, and art institutions. In 2007 she launched Stroll Productions, where she researches, writes, and produces features for print and online publishers including *Departures, Architectural Digest, The New York Post, T: The New York Times Style Magazine, Coastal Living, Interior Design,* and *Cultured.*

Ellen Lupton is curator of contemporary design at the Cooper Hewitt in New York City and director of the Graphic Design MFA program at Maryland Institute College of Art in Baltimore. An AIGA Gold Medalist, she has written numerous books, exhibition catalogs, and articles on design, including the best-selling *Thinking with Type.*

Paul Makovsky is the editorial director of *Metropolis* magazine. He has collaborated on numerous art and design exhibitions and is currently writing a biography of Ward Bennett. He was a Smithsonian Fellow at the Cooper Hewitt.

David Sokol is a New York–based writer whose work focuses on the built environment. He is a contributing editor at *Architectural Record* and *Cultured* and an editorial consultant to multiple design studios and real estate organizations. His books include *Nordic Architects* and *The Modern Architecture Pop-Up Book.*

ACKNOWLEDGMENTS

We are grateful to the designers, artists, and studios who have worked with us since 1997:

AHOY Studios
Morgan Bajardi
Baratloo-Balch Architects
Petra Blaisse
Boym Partners
Desai/Chia Architecture
Mae Engelgeer
Gensler
Michael Graves
Harvard GSD Students
Alexander Isley
karlssonwilker inc.
Myles Karr
Ben Katchor
Graham Kelman
Patty Madden
Charlotte Mann
New Motor

Kari Pei
Karim Rashid
Resistance Design
Anthony Russell
Stefan Sagmeister
Shaw Jelveh Design
David Shields
Snarkitecture
Grethe Sørensen
Laurinda Spear
Christine Tarkowski
Ali Tayar
Tjep.
Tsao & McKown
2x4
Kevin Walz
Carla Weisberg
Elizabeth Whelan

PHOTOGRAPHY CREDITS

All photography © James Shanks unless credited below.

Courtesy AHOY Studios: 159, 160
Andrew Day: 65 bottom, 69, 76 bottom, 99 all except top left
Arman Dowgiert: 68
Courtesy The Guild, karlssonwilker inc.: 174, 180, 186
Hector Guimard, collotype, 1898: 102 inset
Courtesy Inside Outside: 57 inset

Courtesy Kardent Design: 74
Courtesy karlssonwilker inc.: 128 top left, top center, top right, 167, 168, 169, 192
Dan Meyers: 161
Kevin G. Reeves: 75
Marybeth Shaw: 70 top
Christine Tarkowski: 103
Francesca Violetta: 65 top left, 65 top right
Kevin Walz: 64 top right, 64 center right
Courtesy Wolf-Gordon: 12, 72, 73, 76 top, 196–97

Copyright © 2017 by Wolf-Gordon Inc.

All rights reserved.
Published in the United States by Andrea Monfried Editions LLC, New York

Library of Congress Control Number: 2015916210
ISBN 978-0-9910263-4-0

10 9 8 7 6 5 4 3 2 1
First edition

Designed by karlssonwilker inc.
Printed in China

www.andreamonfried.com
CKH ANJ CJ

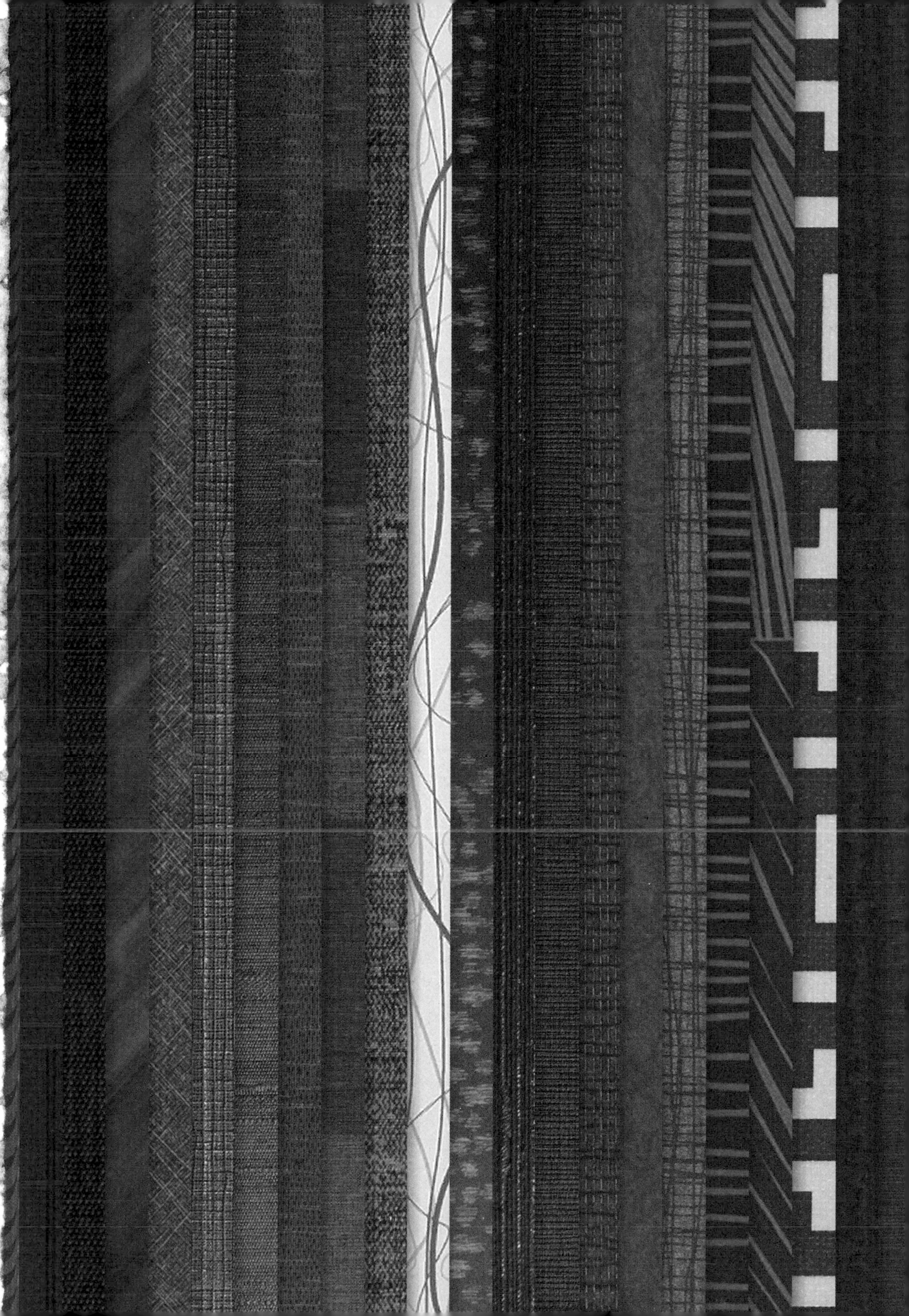